BEHIND ENEMY LINES IN FRANCE AND THE FAR EAST

BEHIND ENEMY LINES IN FRANCE AND THE FAR EAST

SOE AND JEDBURGH OPERATIVE FREDERICK BAILEY, WHO FOUGHT WITH THE RESISTANCE IN EUROPE AND BATTLED THE JAPANESE IN BURMA

MAXINE HARCOURT-KELLY

FRONTLINE BOOKS

First published in Great Britain in 2025
by Frontline Books
An imprint of
Pen & Sword Books Ltd
Yorkshire - Philadelphia

Copyright © Maxine Harcourt-Kelly

ISBN 9 781 03610 646 1

The right of Maxine Harcourt-Kelly to be identified as Author

of this work has been asserted by her in accordance with
the Copyright, Designs and Patents Act 1988.

A CIP catalogue record for this book is available from the British Library

All rights reserved. No part of this book may be reproduced, transmitted, downloaded, decompiled or reverse engineered in any form or by any means, electronic or mechanical including photocopying, recording or by any information storage and retrieval system, without permission from the Publisher in writing. No part of this book may be used or reproduced in any manner for the purpose of training artificial intelligence technologies or systems.

Typeset by Lapiz Digital
Printed and bound in the UK by CPI Group (UK) Ltd,
Croydon, CR0 4YY.

Printed on paper from a sustainable source by
CPI Group (UK) Ltd, Croydon, CR0 4YY

The Publisher's authorised representative in the EU for product safety is Authorised Rep Compliance Ltd., Ground Floor, 71 Lower Baggot Street, Dublin D02 P593, Ireland.
www.arccompliance.com

For a complete list of Pen & Sword titles please contact

PEN & SWORD BOOKS LTD
47 Church Street, Barnsley, South Yorkshire, S70 2AS, England
E-mail: enquiries@pen-and-sword.co.uk
Website: www.pen-and-sword.co.uk

or

PEN & SWORD BOOKS
1950 Lawrence Rd, Havertown, PA 19083, USA
E-mail: uspen-and-sword@casematepublishers.com

Dedicated to the memory of Fred 'The Jed' Bailey and all the Jedburghs - We will remember them.

CONTENTS

Introduction 1

The Early Years 7
Signing Up and Training 21
France 43
Burma and Malaya 79
Post War Life 101
Special Forces Club and Reunions 115
Reflections 127

Appendix 133
    Acknowledgements 133
    Teams despatched from Algiers 133
    Jedburgh Teams despatched from England 150
    Casualties 165
Bibliography 171
Index 175

LIST OF FIGURES

1. Fred around the age of 1 in his beloved Eastbourne
2. Fred at school
3. Fred and family back in Eastbourne
4. Fred at his sister's wedding, far right
5. Team Citroen in Algeria
6. The card Fred carried on him in France, explaining his role
7. Fred outside the Hotel Crillon, Avignon
8. Fred wearing the beret badge that causes much discussion
9. Fred and team in Italy
10. Fred and team in Egypt
11. Sergeant's Mess, Hondona
12. At the Saw Bali Camp, Burma
13. In Burma with one of the elephants, Fred riding on the right
14. The team receiving a drop in Burma
15. Fred and friends at Mount Lavinia Hotel
16. Fred and fellow Jeds enjoying a game of tennis, Ceylon
17. Fred and fellow Jeds at Bentota beach
18. Fred, Tom Henny and another with the car they stole in Kuala Lumpur, 1945
19. Fred on deck, heading home from India in 1946
20. Fred and Sylvia's wedding, 1951
21. Fred with colleagues in his early days at Portsmouth Water Company
22. Fred and Sheila's wedding, 1976
23. Fred on his 60th Birthday with his neighbour retired Commander Hal Eddows in the background
24. The reunion in Paris, at Mount Valerian, 1984
25. Fred and Jed friends in Washington for the American reunion, 1987

26. Fred and friends arriving in Northern France for the 50th anniversary of D-Day
27. Reunion at the *Cutty Sark*, photo courtesy of Simon Leney
28. Reunion at Arundel over a few days, not all who attended in photo, Fred on far right
29. Fred installed as President of Portsmouth and Southsea Rotary Club
30. Pushing the grandchildren up his beloved garden in the early 1990s
31. Fred and Sheila at one of the many social events they attended
32. Meeting Princess Anne at the Natural History Museum, 2015 Photo courtesy of Simon and Kay DeHalpert
33. Receiving the Legion d'Honneur at the D-Day Museum in Portsmouth, 2016
34. Fred's first attendance at the Cenotaph Parade, 2016
35. Fred with his son, John and daughter, Judith at the unveiling of the Lysander replica at Tangmere Military Aviation Museum
36. Fred with the McGregor brothers filming for *RAF at 100*, photo courtesy of Lion Television.
37. Fred with contestants from *Secret Agent Selection and* others at Tangmere Military Aviation Museum
38. Fred again accompanied by his son, John, at the Cenotaph Remembrance Service, 2018
39. Fred
40. Fred on his last birthday, age 99

INTRODUCTION

'I once bought an elephant' so said Fred at dinner one evening.

This sentence brought dinner to an abrupt pause while Fred's grandchildren digested this piece of information. 'Grandpa had an elephant!' Thoughts of Grandpa striding the quiet lanes of Sussex with an elephant were quickly quashed as he proceeded to tell with great humour the story of, in fact, the elephants, plural.

This anecdote told by Fred, laughing uproariously with a glass of wine in his hand, belied the truth of his jungle experiences in Burma during the Second World War.

This is the story of Fred Bailey, my father-in-law, which begins with one man but tells a wider story of a group of men, whose story has often been lost to time, particularly in Britain. Fred would say he was just an ordinary man called to do his duty, and we often agreed that he was, and like many of his generation, they were called to do extraordinary things in wartime. However, as a family we now reflect and perhaps only now realise that actually there was nothing ordinary about him. Of course, to the family he was never ordinary, but this man who would break into a cold sweat at the thought of any DIY did more than any of us will ever know.

The Jedburghs or Jeds as they preferred, ask anyone who they were and few, even now, will be able to tell you. Briefly, they were three-man teams parachuted into occupied Europe, behind enemy lines. Their role was to co-ordinate the Resistance and assist the advancing allied forces, using whatever resources to thwart the Germans. But this is too simplistic an explanation.

There seems, in some areas, to be the belief that they were American, but this was a British conceived idea within the Special Operations Executive. It was brought to life with the co-operation and involvement of the United States and those French who wanted to free their country but it was British in origin. There was often friction between the British and the United States once the US entered the war, with one conversation between President Roosevelt and Oliver Stanley quoted - Roosevelt 'I do not want to be unkind or rude to the British, but in 1841, when you acquired Hong Kong, you did not acquire it by purchase.' To which Stanley responded 'Let me see, Mr President, that was about the time of the Mexican war, wasn't it?'.[1] This conversation in January 1945 shows that these close allies maintained a certain friction especially in the Far East. In spite of this the Jedburghs are one shining example of international cooperation between the British and Americans and French in particular.

It is, nonetheless, true to say that the United States ran with the idea and the Jedburghs are viewed as the founding fathers of the Green Berets with the American Office of Strategic Sevices (OSS) leading to the post war birth of the CIA. The CIA website gives a reasonable account of the Jeds, although no mention is made of Colonel Holland, Colonel Grand or M1 (R), whose early exploits gave the germ of the idea for the Jedburghs. It is General (at the time) Gubbins who is generally credited with the idea which would become the Jedburghs, although he credits Peter Wilkinson. Certainly the Americans took what they considered the best of the British Special Forces and developed their own structure which continues to this day and this is clearly where the idea that they were American comes from. The British, on the other hand, have quietly left the Jedburghs in the past with little reference or acknowledgment to their work. The SAS born around the same time took the mantle of the secret force, while MI6 and other MI divisions were already in place, so the SOE and with it the Jedburghs were allowed to quietly sink into an all too secret history.

Eisenhower and Churchill both saw the value of the idea of the Jedburghs. An agreement was reached which saw British Jedburghs recruited and trained in England and Scotland, while US members were initially trained on their home turf. Eventually all met in England. French Jedburghs were recruited - mostly from North Africa, where following the liberation there were many French soldiers wanting to fight for their home.

Fred and his fellow colleagues were part of the Special Operations Executive (hereinafter SOE), a department few in the regular forces even knew existed. This was a branch formed to carry out ungentlemanly warfare, guerrilla warfare with an aim to assist those resisting in occupied territories. They sent men and many women in behind the enemy lines, to organise and report on Resistance activities

---

1   Jim Lacey, Ed. *Great Strategic Rivalries: From the Classical World to the Cold War*, United Kingdom, Oxford University Press, 2016, p. 361

and to encourage those activities. Many men and women of the SOE died unknown, some names today are known a little Violet Szabo, Noor Inyat Khan and a few of the men, but too few are remembered, particularly in Great Britain.

For decades Fred could not speak of his service, but from the mid-1980s the veil of secrecy was gradually pulled back and suddenly here were these men and in the wider SOE, women who worked behind enemy lines, harassing the enemy and aiding the Resistance across Europe and ultimately laying the path for the allied troops as they moved into Europe. These unsung heroes, who could never parade past the Cenotaph as Jedburghs, quietly lived their lives post war, even when allowed to speak of their experiences, they spoke sparingly and with great caution.

Something had actually been known if you knew where to look. As early as 1947 a film *Now It Can Be Told* gave an account of the SOE, and the incredible work of their agents, yet the Jedburghs are not included.[2] The great historian M R D Foot wrote the history of the SOE in the 1960s, being granted special access to still-secret papers and certainly discussed this select band of soldiers. But his tome of work informed historians and did not appear to reach a wider audience, who remained blissfully unaware. Due to his restricted access though several threatened libel action, the full story was not in official papers.

The SOE and its place in history has been written about extensively but remains slightly obscure. The Jedburgh position within SOE and the wider history of the Second World War remains elusive to a wider audience. While the Americans will point to it being the forerunner of their Green Berets, Britain cannot point to an equivalent, in 1940 France under Free French Captain Georges Bergé had founded their own Special Forces in London, while in exile, whose name and motto mirrored the UK's SAS.

This book will not deal with the wider SOE but will focus on Fred Bailey, a radio operator who wanted to do his bit for the war, and like all the Jedburghs is owed a debt of gratitude that was not always forthcoming, simply because they were unknown.

The purpose of this book is to hold a light to the extraordinary work that a small select group of men did during the Second World War. There were many women who ensured that this group of men were both trained and supported through their deployment, working under

---

2   Teddy Baird, Dir. *Now it can be told*, 1947

the banner of the First Aid Nursing Yeomanry (FANY), a misnomer as many worked in communications and were support staff. They were held in the highest regard by the Jedburghs both at the time and in the decades that followed.

During the Second World War, men and women across nations stepped up and did what they felt they had to do. They did it for their country, for its people and for their own families. Some feel we know all we can about the war, but pockets of secrecy remain and frankly will remain locked in the past. By the very nature of secret operations, those who take part cannot or will not talk and even today there will be aspects of the Second World War that we will never know.

In discussion with the family, we know Fred would be pleased that a book is shining a light on the Jedburghs. While incredibly humble, in his later years, he appreciated the attention he received and that in his own small way he was able to tell something of his war experiences and remind the world that the Jedburghs existed, although he was always surprised that anyone was interested. Nonetheless, the one thing Fred always said was that he had experienced and endured so that no-one else had to and for that reason he only gave what we consider a sanitised, almost scripted, version of events.

In researching this book, I have recalled the many conversations Fred and I had over the years and delved into the archives. I have watched and listened to the many interviews Fred and other Jedburghs gave, as well as many books written about the Resistance, the SOE and the Jedburghs. There are also many academic theses written about the Jedburghs, usually by American military men undertaking further education. The advantage some, including myself, have had is that they were able to speak to many while they were still alive. Keggie Carew, daughter of Tom Carew, has written with extraordinary candour about her family and in turn the experiences of those that served. Harry Verlander's memoir among others gives us further details and sometimes information that Fred did not share. Simon Leney, son of Roger Leney, shared his father's as yet unpublished memoir of his time in Burma. I have also worked from the official records at the National Archives in Kew, often to check information and also to glean fuller details, where possible. I have listened to Fred's interview held at the Imperial War Museum as well as others, particularly Martyn Cox's interview with Fred on Legasee. I am indebted to Martyn Cox and the Legasee Project, which recorded so many veterans including Fred so that their stories can be told and remembered. It has been particularly bittersweet to watch Fred chatting in the Legasee video, which was shot in his living room. It is worth noting that it was at least 40 years before any of the Jeds could discuss their service, so here and there you find some discrepancies, usually around dates or the order of things. It has therefore been necessary, where possible, to recheck events against official sources as well as attempting to find corroborating testimony.

Fred's post war life was measured, successful and without doubt happy. His background was straight forward, a happy family, a good childhood combined with a good education. Yet it is, in many ways, the very ordinariness of his life that makes him exceptional. I had the good fortune to know him for over 40 years, he had a laugh that lit up the room, he loved his gin and bitter lemon, a good boxing match and cricket. The kindly gentle man that I met when he was in his early 50s belied the truth of what had shaped him as a young man.

While the book will give an overview of the Jedburgh role throughout France, its focus will be on the south. This is where Fred Bailey found himself deployed in August 1944 as part of Team Citroen. After France, Fred had an interesting visit to Italy followed ultimately by deployment with Force 136 to Burma and Malaya.

Fred was a radio operator, vital for the team, but he was not a swash buckling hero. He was, like so many, just there to see some action and do his job and if he was lucky, get home to enjoy a life of freedom and peace. The very nature of the Special Forces mean that you find some interesting characters along the way and certainly the SOE and the Jedburghs had their fair share, but it also had those that might be described as ordinary, who simply did their job and then, for the fortunate ones, got on with enjoying their lives.

Fred Bailey, was I believe, the last Jedburgh, he died in January 2023 taking with him many secrets and his famous Welsh rarebit recipe and as a family we are probably more upset about the rarebit recipe.

CHAPTER ONE

THE EARLY YEARS

Fred was born at number 29 Granville Square, Clerkenwell, London on 20 November 1923; his army records often get this wrong and make him a year younger. His family were Londoners, actually Cockneys, through and through.[3] A look through his family history shows the family located around City Road for years with mentions of Essex and Kent several generations back. A proud cockney family, Fred was appreciative of his roots, if a tad disappointed that there didn't seem to be any adventurers who had strayed far from London. People flocked to where the work was and the generations leading to Fred would have found work easier to find in the city than in more rural areas.

The London that Fred was born into was very different to the city today. Inner London, where Fred lived had a population of just under 5 million. The Great War of 1914-1918 was still fresh in the mind and there was a blossoming of industry around London. The influence of the United States was felt during the inter war years. The hangover of the Victorians clung on in some areas but modernisation was rumbling ahead when Fred was born. His parents must have thought he was born in a golden age, the Great War - the war to end all wars - was behind them and in 1923 no-one envisaged another war, industries were booming thanks in large part to the recent availability of electricity.

When Fred was one year old the British Empire Exhibition was held at Wembley, promoting the trade of the Empire and over the course of one year welcomed around 25 million visitors.[4] This was still a time of Empire, but times were already changing with anti-colonial sentiment

---

3   A cockney is someone born with the sound of Bow Bells in the City of London, the city sits within the wider known area of London

4   British Empire Exhibition, National Archives, CO 323/922/45 among other files

growing. The Great War had moved Britain from a powerful nation to one that was in substantial debt, particularly to the rising power of the United States and financially it needed the Empire. Fred's father, also Frederick, had been born in 1887 and married Dora Merriman in 1913, he worked as a gas meter collector. This was someone who would call at houses and empty the cash from the meter for the local company. This was a time when women found their roles very slowly shifting. Fred's mother worked as a shorthand typist, in fact she was one of the first in London, a fact Fred was always very proud of and would often tell people. Dora was one of a generation of women who were realising a life beyond domestic jobs previously available. It had only been four years since some women were granted the right to vote and it would be 1928 before voting was open to all women. Frederick senior was one of fourteen children, Dora was one of four children, although she lost one brother during the First World War in France in 1916.

During Fred's early years the population of London grew as new industries from the United States moved in, from vacuum cleaning company Hoover to Firestone, the tyre company, the Great West Road filled with new industries.

But the young Fred was oblivious to all this, born into a happy home, Granville Square was and is a square of substantial properties. Fred would play with his sister as well as cousins who lived on the opposite side of the square. He fondly remembered his little red firetruck which he used to ride around the square as a small child. At the time there was a church within the square where only a garden now sits. The Church had been built in 1831/2 by Edward Buckton Lamb, not the most popular architect, often referred to as a rogue Gothic Revivalist. The area had been countryside until developed as part of the Lloyd Baker Estate. The church was demolished in 1938, years after Fred and his family had moved away. Fred's older sister, Dora, to whom he was very close, despite their nine-year age gap, would sadly pass away far too early at the age of 54 in 1968, her loss remained with him. He took great pleasure in watching her family grow and have families themselves and he remained close to them.

As a young child Fred suffered from a heart condition, myocarditis, which is an enlargement of the heart. From the age of three to six, Fred spent much of his time in bed, either at home or in hospital. The family physician finally recommended that the family move away from the London clay and they relocated to Hertfordshire, the Bushey-Watford area, Oxhey specifically. This may seem a short simple move today, but it must have been quite an upheaval for this family to move from an area they were so associated with. Fred's health was excellent after this move, so clearly the advice was good. This interesting situation was repeated when his grandson had asthma and Fred's stepson and family were advised to move to improve the health of their son.

Family holidays to Eastbourne were a favourite and Fred held very happy memories of childhood visits to the town, travelling by train to the seaside was a visit millions took every year. Fred visited regularly throughout his life there was a boyish joy when he returned, the years melted away and you could see the happy memories playing behind his eyes. Fish and chips and an ice cream on the front were, for Fred, throughout his life, a great day out. Indeed ice cream was the only dessert Fred was ever interested in and he took great pleasure in a bowl of vanilla ice cream, only vanilla, regardless of where in the world he was.

Fred loved sport, playing it as a youngster, watching it as an older man, and was a fan of Watford FC from a young age and kept the faith with them throughout his life. He forgave his stepson John for getting married on the one day that Watford made it to the FA cup final. They had always said they would go to Wembley if Watford ever got there. Beyond football he loved cricket as well as boxing, he loved seeing two men knock the stuffing out of each other and would roar with laughter, while shouting encouragement at the television.

He seems to have enjoyed school, which was Hemel Hempstead Grammar. At the time Fred was in school, it was normal to work towards a School Certificate, this meant you needed to pass at least six subjects to complete. A letter from the school, dated 17 January 1940, states that had the war not interfered with his education he would have achieved a good result and completed his education.[5] The letter makes mention of his good appearance, a pleasant disposition and that he is thoroughly honest and reliable. A reflection of the times this was written in, it also states he is well built, of good physique and excellent general health. This final comment is very satisfying when one considers just how poorly he was as a small child. Fred stated that he matriculated out of school, which was an exemption based on having completed a good proportion of his school course. He was a member of the school cricket team and apparently was keenly interested in drama. While history was his favourite subject, he recalled the lady teacher with a certain affection, so one suspects it might have been her that

---

5   Personal papers of Fred Bailey

inspired his love of the subject. Throughout his life Fred always had an eye for a pretty lady, even towards the end of his life, the familiar twinkle would appear in his eyes if a lady walked into the room.

War was declared on 3 September 1939, two days after Germany invaded Poland. Fred, still fifteen at the time, was too young to join up, but found ways to support the war effort at home.

Having left school, he initially joined an insurance company which had evacuated from London. He became a fire picket at work and an ARP warden messenger and member of the Home Guard, he felt fully immersed in the war even before he hit the age of sixteen.

He wasn't very keen on the job in insurance, he always said he didn't see a future in it. Anthony Blackwell, of the Crosse and Blackwell company, whom Fred referred to as the local squire, gave some assistance and he was offered a job at the Colne Valley Water Company.[6] Anthony Blackwell and his family had owned Oxhey Place since 1877 and it seems he took an active interest in those who lived in the area. Sadly, Anthony would be killed while on active service in 1942 with the estate being compulsory purchased two years later.

Fred in his own words 'jumped at the chance of joining the water company'. He began training for professional qualifications with the Chartered Institute of Secretaries, which would lead to a company secretary qualification while working as a wages clerk. He had completed the preliminary training by the time he joined up at the age of 18. This was a time when you were expected to choose a career early and stick with it for life. However, things were not going to be so straight forward for Fred or his generation.

As soon as he could, on his 18th birthday Fred signed up, this was November 1941. He had seen two years of war on the home front and youthful enthusiasm meant Fred, like so many young men, could not wait to see some action and do their bit for King and country. This was, of course, a difficult time for everyone but for his mother, Dora, having lost a brother in the First World War this must have been especially difficult.

While Fred was eager to join up and see some action, others had been working for years to find a less conventional way of dealing with the enemy.

---

6   Crosse and Blackwell, a condiment company was originally formed in 1706 – Crosse and Blackwell were two apprentices who bought the company in 1830. It secured one of the first royal warrants from Queen Victoria. Today the brand is simply a name within a global conglomerate having changed hands multiple times.

SOE

The Special Operations Executive, formed in 1940 and often attributed to Winston Churchill, was in fact signed off by Neville Chamberlain.

For the purposes of this work, it is perhaps necessary to start before the Second World War and consider what Europe was experiencing just twenty short years after the Great War. The Great Flu Epidemic or as it's more widely known, Spanish Flu had then travelled the world killing millions in the two years following the Great War. The Spanish Civil War was ongoing, Hitler had occupied Austria and was eyeing Czechoslovakia with fascism spreading within and across Europe.

With the 'fifth column' idea already in use within Europe, it was obvious for British minds to turn to the idea of a subversive war as well as the more traditional offensive/defensive war.[7]

Of course, intelligence had been used since time began in varying guises both within Britain and beyond. Indeed, the use of intelligence is even shown in the bible. Additionally in Britain, the royal family had a long history of intelligence, using their European family connections ensured they tended to be very well informed.

Subversion and propaganda were not new tools, and the idea of irregular warfare was also not new, one can go back through history to find instances of irregular warfare. It has been a factor throughout the world through time but the escapades of T E Lawrence, the famed Lawrence of Arabia is one of the most famous from the First World War and could be drawn upon in the most recent past as well as Northcliffe, who had proved useful in America.[8] Added to that, the troubles in Ireland, as well as the Boer War meant that, in particular, Churchill was familiar with the idea and a great proponent of the idea of irregular warfare, he had seen it at work.

So against this background of civil war and incitement across Europe, there were some within the British establishment that were keeping a keen eye and began to prepare for what they could see as another potential war in Europe.

There were several small departments, all looking at various options to be used during wartime, from propaganda to guerrilla warfare. The

---

7 The fifth column was the idea that subversive forces worked in a country preparing it and influencing the public to favour the Nazi idea. Propaganda and subversion were used within a country to undermine a country's population and their unity.

8 Lawrence of Arabia, a British Intelligence officer who worked with Arab guerilla forces during the First World War. Alfred Harmsworth, Viscount Northcliffe, a newspaper owner who exerted great influence was made Director of Propaganda and led a mission to the US.

overriding impression is that there was clear overlap and also little organisation or oversight on these various departments. These were Section D, Electra House and MI(R), GSR.[9] Taking these in turn, Section D, originally Section IX, of the Secret Intelligence Service was formed in late 1938 at the same time as Lord Halifax of the Foreign Office was forming Electra House. Major Lawrence Grand, a dapper chap with a quick wit, was brought in to run Section D. He was instructed to think about anything that could weaken an enemy from within, from literal sabotage to the more subtle moral sabotage of a population. This was, of course, peacetime, so his first report, restricted, it seems, to the intelligence service, caused some nervousness around the potential for diplomatic incidents, should currently friendly nations discover plans to sabotage them. Nonetheless, Section D was not insignificant, ultimately with personnel in multiple countries, it was a department of spies.

Electra House was the second small unit formed under the supposed control of the Foreign Office. Yet organisation was shambolic, with little clear direction. It came into being in January 1939 as an Enemy Publicity Section, with an initial approach to Sir Campbell Stuart during the Munich crisis in 1938. He had enjoyed a close association with Crewe House during the First World War, famed for its use of propaganda, and seemed the obvious choice to head this new section. The immediate issue was that the Ministry of Information had its own division of enemy and enemy occupied countries department which was tasked with not just collecting information but looking at propaganda and counter propaganda. Throw the BBC into the mix and there were multiple arms who felt they had roles to play. However, Electra House set up radio broadcasts to be sent into the enemy countries yet purporting to be from rebels within. They also printed material to appear as if it was German for distribution. Section D also apparently did this. These small ideas and initial attempts would prove very useful and effective later in the war, particularly in France where the idea and implementation of underground newspapers by the Resistance played a useful role.

By no means least the MI (R) department, which began as the GS (R) department, in 1938 a statement in the House of Commons referred to its role as purely military research, a small section to study warfare. By December of that year Colonel J F C Holland was placed in charge, a man with experience both in Ireland and India of the irregular nature that warfare could take.

---

9   M R D Foot, *SOE in France*, London: Her Majesty's Stationery Office, 1966, p.xvii

Both Section D and MI (R) worked physically close initially and joint proposals in March 1939 reflected both Holland and Grand and moved at pace. A paper was prepared for the Chief of the Imperial General Staff, followed swiftly a few days later with a meeting between the Chief of the Imperial General Staff, the Foreign Secretary, a Foreign Office official and Permanent Under Secretary Cadogan. Between them they agreed to secretly move to counter Nazi influence in countries it was threatening or where it already had a foothold.

This was taken further in June 1940 with a small incursion by three officers into France. They landed by trawler and then rowed back to England, taking 13 hours for their return trip. There is little information on this event, but it showed that what were referred to as 'mosquito' raids by small groups of men could be carried out. Section D, before the fall of France, had even managed to secrete ten small amounts of sabotage material across 150 miles of northern France. They left each supply in the care of 2 Frenchmen, but without advice or strategy, this came to nothing but again suggested the seeds of both Resistance and aiding resistors.

These small independent sections would be the foundation for the SOE, although their very nature and structure meant that they all but disappeared. These early sections and the work they did should not be underestimated, they bore fruit, had well trained individuals and planted the seeds for many future successes.

Yet the absolute issue is the obvious one, clandestine activities need to be kept secret and small sections all reporting to different departments ensured a level of disorganisation, duplication and risk.

The move to a cohesive organisation took some time but was recognised by Section D as early as June 1939. Ultimately it was in May 1940 that an urgency to matters arose with the crumbling of the front and the evacuation from Dunkirk. The chiefs of staff stated that even if France fell, Germany could be defeated 'by economic pressure, by a combination of air attack on economic objectives in Germany and on German morale and the creation of widespread revolt in her conquered territories.'[10] They suggested a special organisation would be necessary. Meetings and papers swirled, but Churchill got behind the idea with enthusiasm and with the fall of France called in Maurice Hankey (Chancellor of the Duchy of Lancaster) to co-ordinate and organise these separate groups. Various struggles between departments continued until Lord Halifax called a decisive meeting on 1 July at

---

10 M R D Foot, *SOE in France*, London: Her Majesty's Stationery Office, 1966, p. 6

the Foreign Office. Finally on 16 July 1940 Churchill appointed Hugh Dalton, the Minister for Economic Warfare and the SOE was born.

Hugh Dalton, the minister of economic warfare said of SOE's role;

> We have got to organise movements in enemy occupied territory comparable to the Sinn Fein movement in Ireland, to the Chinese Guerrillas operating against Japan, to the Spanish Irregulars who played a notable part in Wellington's campaign or one might as well admit it - to the organisations which the nazis themselves have developed so remarkably in almost every country in the world. This 'democratic international' must use many different methods, including industrial and military sabotage, labour agitation and strikes, continuous propaganda, terrorist acts agains traitors and German leaders, boycotts and riots.[11]

The idea was therefore set and work could begin to, as Churchill apparently said, 'Set Europe Ablaze'. This is a tad dramatic but does convey the idea.

It was though, Chamberlain, the former Prime Minister who handled the details for Churchill. It was one of his final acts before his death. Having resigned and advising the King to bring in Churchill in May, he had remained in parliament and had encouraged his Conservative Party to support Churchill, which was something of a challenge.[12]

It was interesting that Churchill used Dalton to oversee the SOE initially, they were not friends at all, but Churchill recognised in spite of their very different political views that Dalton was the right man for the job, at least initially.

The most important person drafted into the new organisation was Colin Gubbins, a soldier of note, who had written several booklets which would form the basis of much SOE training. It was not an easy appointment, and it required Churchill's personal intervention to get Gubbins in post.

General Gubbins, as he was at this point, had served in the First World War, Russia, India, Northern Ireland, giving him an extensive level of experience both in conventional and unconventional warfare. He had been brought in initially at Holland's request to MI(R) and wrote what started as a handbook but turned into three separate booklets, about A5 in size. They were *The Art of Guerrilla Warfare, How to Use High Explosives* and *Partisan Leader's Handbook*. These would be translated

---

11   Foot, *SOE in France*, p.8

12   Ibid

into several languages, particularly the work on high explosives, and would be effective for agents and resisters throughout Europe.[13]

The idea was very much based on the ideas of organisations such as Sinn Fein, Spanish irregulars and Chinese guerrillas - it was about encouraging those on the ground to cause disruption and damage - yet for those people to melt safely away. Indeed, the SOE were often referred to as the Baker Street Irregulars, so named after their offices in Central London.

Gubbins would be promoted to Brigadier in this new organisation. The SOE, while starting from these various strands, built into a significant force with agents throughout Europe. There were SOE operatives from Norway to Yugoslavia, and in the Far East with relevant section heads and departments in London. While a good number came from a military background, SOE did not rely on the military for their personnel. The very nature of the work they undertook meant that those from a military background might not be the most suitable. These people had to blend in, think on their feet and often were brought in due to their local knowledge or specialist skills. A case in point is Maurice Buckmaster, in charge of F Section (France).[14] While he was in the military during the war, his background was in France working for the Ford Motor Company. This gave him the advantage of knowing and understanding the manufacturing business in France which in turn meant he knew where sabotage would be most useful. There was even a safe breaker collected from prison on his release and recruited into SOE. Men and women were dropped behind enemy lines to help organise sabotage, assist and guide the Resistance and send intelligence back to London.

For France, the scope was clear but also it presented the challenge that the country was split in two, between the occupied and the unoccupied. When it came to the efforts of the SOE in terms of sabotage, there were differences in approach between the two zones of France. Official papers discuss this quite clearly, stating that in the north it was quite reasonable for discreet explosions to occur, but in the unoccupied south, fires might mysteriously light but things could not go bang in the night.[15] The subtleties between the occupied north and the unoccupied south are worth considering, agents who were well trained found themselves at a loss in the early days of SOE, instructions were vague and often agents were in place but not entirely sure how to

---

13 Brian Lett, *SOE's Mastermind*, Barnsley: Pen and Sword Military, 2016, p. 89
14 Maurice Buckmaster, *They Fought Alone*, London: Biteback, 2014
15 National Archives

proceed. Instructions of insaisissable (elusive) sabotage, discreet bangs and organising resistance were vague terms which did not aid those early agents.

As time went on, the skill of these agents was tested in terms of diplomacy beyond their original anticipated role. Official documents reflect that they were there to aid with sabotage whereas any guerrilla warfare or uprising was purely in French hands, but of course the lines blurred and both intelligence and guerrilla actions were engaged with. There are many well known agents from SOE. Often some of the female agents are highlighted to show that women were heavily involved and were dying, often tortuous deaths, for the freedom of Europe.

The successes of the circuits should not be underestimated, in time many were very successful. Railway lines were sabotaged across the country, causing untold disruption to the movement of troops and equipment, factories were disabled and Allied personnel were aided in their escape and as the war progressed, the railway sabotage took on a further urgency it was hoped to halt the deportation of many to the death camps.

The SOE was already active in France before De Gaulle's BCRA, Bureau Central de Renseignements et d'Action, was up and running in mid 1941, before Fred had even joined up. Naturally, the French wanted full control over any subversive activity in France, but the British were alarmed at the apparent lack of security with the French, demonstrated with an abortive action in Dakar, leading to the British keeping firm hold of the reins. French and British circuits would work independently of each other in France, but De Gaulle was completely dependent on the British for training, equipment and transport, which worked through the RF section of SOE. Naturally there were difficulties and obstructions to two separate organisations working towards the same goal in the same country, but there were advantages as well. For one thing, the Germans were constantly chasing two organisations, both well trained and equipped. For the British, there was a very clear non-political status, they were not interested in getting embroiled in any local or wider political debate. Although they cared deeply about France and were not remotely keen on Pétain and the idea of a Nazi satellite state.

The agents of SOE were a varied bunch from a variety of backgrounds so the French could engage with the pure aim of freeing their country. There were though multiple political issues, differing Resistance groups and particularly the communist resisters who wanted a communist country at the end of the war, often there was a need for diplomacy to keep all the groups focused on the enemy rather than each other. The various Resistance circuits though were not supposed to know of each other's existence, one thread that ran across the various Resistance organisations was the need to compartmentalise, the less they knew the better for all. Agents from SOE would not know who or if there was another agent nearby. They assimilated into local life and hid in plain sight, for example, George Starr was made deputy mayor in Castelnau-sous-l'Auvignon, such was his success. There were though instances where crossovers occurred, one agent who was repeatedly chastised for travelling around too much was Henri Sevenet, who ran the Detective circuit. He travelled widely imparting training in sabotage but was warned he could be caught. His Montagne Noir force was very successful in sabotage but as a result eventually drew the attention of the enemy and an air-raid on their position killed Sevenet and many others.[16] Another recorded event was when two agents saw each other at a train station, one behaved properly - completely ignoring the person they knew from training. The other agent though made a few attempts to gain the attention of the other agent before realising the danger.[17]

It was not plain sailing for the SOE and it took some time for them to find their feet. One issue for anyone associated with SOE was that there was departmental squabbling and perhaps even jealousy. The MI sections were still in their relative infancy and did not take kindly to this wartime upstart, in fact they insisted it was to be closed at the end of the war. The muddled command structure and absolute secrecy around SOE and its branches have led to many myths and errors over the years. Much has been written about the SOE and those who served, but it's important to say that in spite of its early problems, it played an increasingly important, if very secret, part in the war.

The Jedburghs were conceived by the SOE and would be part of the organisation. Due to their position outside the traditional military there's a certain mysticism surrounding the Jedburghs. A secret small group of around 300. I had the pleasure of being the daughter-in-law to one former radio operator.

The Jedburghs may be viewed as having had something of a challenger in the guise of the SAS, founded within the military in 1941. The SAS was considered a strike force, effective and deadly, they aimed to get into a situation, deal with it and remove themselves

---

16 Nigel Atkins and Jan Christensen, *Secret Operations over Occupied Europe*, Barnsley: Pen and Sword, 2024, p. 54

17 Foot, *SOE in France*, p.112

swiftly. However, the Jedburghs regarded themselves above this, they could no doubt be effective and deadly but there was something else which has led to them being referred to as diplomat-soldiers and Paul McCue has referred to them as a cerebral group of men, which seems apt.[18] They could kill without hesitation if needed but they could talk situations down as well. Their role was more one of embedding with Resistance forces and aiding them, through training and leadership. However, the CIA does list their motto as Surprise, Kill, Vanish, which they were clearly capable of.[19]

Part of the issue around a lack of awareness, apart from the obvious secrecy, was that SOE comprised of so few relative to the war effort. People can name beaches and talk about D-Day, but they are often completely unaware that the SOE with their agents and the Jedburgh section as well as the SAS and Special Forces from the United States and France, were there behind enemy lines, deep behind, working and in many cases dying to stop the Germans sending reinforcements to the north and the beaches.

The 32 special qualities required to be a Jedbugh.[20]

1. His civilian record is impressive
2. He will be a good fighting soldier
3. He will make a good organiser
4. He can command others
5. He will be popular with his associates
6. He has a personality which will impress others
7. He is considerate of others
8. He will cooperate well
9. He is tactful
10. He has stability of temperament
11. He is thoroughly reliable
12. He has a good sense of discipline
13. He will retain a steady morale throughout
14. He has self-confidence
15. He can take decisions decisively
16. He will have enthusiasm for the work
17. He has plenty of personal initiative

---

18 Lt. Col. Will Irwin (Ret), *The Jedburghs*, United States: Public Affairs, 2005, p.xxiv, Paul McCue, Trustee WW2 Secret Learning Network.
19 CIA Website, Surprise-Kill-Vanish-The-Legend-Of-The-Jedburghs
20 National Archives, HS7-18

18. He is capable of acting independently
19. He welcomes responsibility
20. He is capable of assuming responsibility
21. He is an aggressive active type
22. He has good planning ability
23. He is a very practical sort of man
24. He is a man of the world
25. He will be determined and will persevere
26. He is clear thinking
27. He uses his intelligence to best advantage
28. He is fond of risk and adventure
29. He has good physical stamina
30. He is physically agile
31. His motivation is sound
32. He is a man of integrity

CHAPTER TWO

SIGNING UP AND TRAINING

While SOE was being established, the young Fred couldn't wait to join up on his 18th birthday. Fred's parents, like so many, accepted their son joining up with a mixture of pride and fear.

Fred joined the army, volunteering for active service in the Royal Armoured Corps. He recalled the sense of the whole country being involved and convinced that victory was inevitable. He was young, full of enthusiasm and keen to contribute and be part of the victory. Like many, Fred volunteered rather than wait to be called up. In doing so, this allowed some control over deployment, you could choose your unit rather than being assigned to a unit you might feel ill suited to. This had been his argument when discussing volunteering with his parents.

He chose the Royal Armoured Corps as, at the point of joining up, the war in the North African desert was ongoing and Fred liked the idea of being in the midst of the action. One can imagine the youthful exuberance of these young men, keen to serve and so confident in the country's ability to defeat the evil of Nazism. Although it is fair to say that Fred more than once said there were times when victory seemed distant and in no way guaranteed.[21]

He was initially posted to Bovington in Dorset, training as a radio operator and gunner, learning Morse code, as well as gunnery training. Six months later he deployed to The Green Howards, 13th battalion. Fred always said this was one of his bad decisions, having volunteered he had a certain degree in choice as to where he was posted. This had been an infantry battalion but converted to an armoured car regiment and was based in Scarborough. While he had hoped to be deployed to a tank regiment, he recognised that the war was moving at a pace

---

21 Personal Comms.

and was initially pleased with the move to Scarborough. He felt an armoured car regiment would get to see some action.

However, his pleasure was short lived. He recounted in pretty much every interview, as well as when speaking with family, how disappointed he was in the Green Howards. In his words he found the commanding officers a dead loss and most of the ranks, mostly conscripts and not very keen ones, were just interested in getting their next leave rather than going into the war. For a young man, who had volunteered and was eager to do his bit, he was despondent and desperate to improve his options. The first issue was that there were hardly any armoured cars, so it was clear that there was going to be an issue there.

Fred was with three other friends from Bovington in Scarborough and it seems that almost from the moment they arrived they tried to move on to anything other than the Green Howards. Fred said none of them minded the thought of dying for their country, but if they were going to die they wanted to die being useful. They felt staying with the Green Howards might mean a pointless death and none of them were prepared for that.

It seems they applied with gusto to special units, whether Paras, glider pilots or anything that offered a potential escape from the Green Howards.

While Fred and his comrades wallowed with the Green Howards, in May 1942, Gubbins met with the DCGS and CCO to discuss the idea of Anglo-American operations.[22] Official papers recall this meeting set out the germ of the idea for the Jedburghs.

'As and when invasion commences SOE will drop additional small teams of French speaking personnel carrying arms for some forty men each. The role of these teams will be to make contact with local authorities or existing SOE organisations, to distribute the arms, to start off the action of the patriots, and, most particularly, to arrange by W/T communication the dropping points and reception committees for further arms and equipment on the normal SOE system. Each team will consist of one British officer, one W/T operator with set and possibly one guide'.[23]

---

22 National Archives HS7/17, DCGS - Deputy Chief General Staff, CCO - Chief of Combined Operations

23 Ibid

Peter Wilkinson is credited by Gubbins, after he produced a paper in 1942, but the predecessors of SOE had also planted the initial seed for the idea.[24]

By July 1942 the name Jedburgh had been assigned to this idea. The name causes a lot of debate but the simple and most logical reason for the name is that it was simply the next name on a list. It was said that the name Jumpers was suggested when the request was sent in, so that may have influenced a name beginning with J, but that is pure speculation. The Inter Services Security Board had a list of names and a request would be put in for a name and back one would come a couple of days later. It is said that Churchill took great interest in the assigning of code names and that he liked to review and approve them. Planning was taking place at this stage with the main agreement being that the Americans would provide half the required number of men and the British the rest. Some initial discussions as to numbers was also discussed with the number of teams suggested at 70, but no firm decisions as to numbers or even firm locations that they could be used in were finalised at this stage. The SOE though was working to a timetable and assuming that an invasion of France could take place anytime from the autumn of 1943.

At this point in time, when the idea took shape, communications and knowledge of the Resistance was limited. It was assumed that the Jedburghs would be vital to communications and training of the Resistance, it was felt that any full-scale invasion would rely on the Jedburghs embedding in the occupied territories. However, as the war progressed and the work of SOE developed, communications and training advanced and would ultimately impact the role of the Jedburghs. It was around this time that Peter Wilkinson delivered a paper on the Jedburgh idea and Gubbins ran with it.

Following a meeting in December 1942, it was decided that it would be necessary to both test the idea and use the opportunity to garner support for the idea of the Jedburghs. Operation Spartan was planned; it would take place across the English countryside and while there was a realisation that using the RAF to drop troops would be unlikely due to other demands, they would be able to pinpoint drop zones for supplies.[25] The teams to be used in Spartan would not be Jeds but SOE personnel and the villagers to assist them would be other personnel drawn from the military. It was carried out in March 1943

---

24 Brian Lett, *SOE's Mastermind*, p.232

25 Ibid

and deemed a success, those observing being encouraged by the idea of the Jedburghs. The French and Belgian observers were convinced that the Jedburghs had value. The OSS had sent two majors from America along to observe and they were appropriately enthused and took the idea back to Washington where ultimately recruitment of the necessary numbers of American personnel could take place. Further decisions were made following Spartan, one was the realisation that the commander or second in command of each team should be from the country the team were being dropped to, additionally they would all be soldiers (unlike SOE) and that they would wear uniforms. This decision to wear uniforms would leave no doubt should they be captured as to who they were and certainly placed an added danger on the Jedburghs. On the other hand it also had the advantage that when they dealt with the Resistance members, it was clear as to who they were and that they were there to help. It was felt that the teams would need up to 3 days to organise themselves once dropped in, so any demands on them should allow for this settlement time. While it was planned that they would drop to areas where SOE already had agents in place, they would be allocated certain tasks clearly aimed at furthering the military aims within a specified region. It was appreciated that any teams too close to the German front line would struggle to work with local groups due to enemy survellience, so was therefore realised that they would have to be further back. Some reports state they would need to be at least 40 miles behind enemy lines and that while operating in that theatre it could be some time before they would be reached by the allied forces. It is at this point that those in charge began to realise that the Jedburghs would be a strategic force. They would be able to tackle lines of communication, headquarters and any legitimate target from a guerrilla warfare aspect, but primarily transport and military targets.

It was likewise realised that small groups of paratroopers, such as the SAS, would be suited to surprise attacks on the enemy but that the Jedburghs would be more suited to lying low and working with the resistance in a more prolonged way. It would be their role to supply and train resisters, provide radio communications and if there were issues with a lack of leadership within the resisters to provide such leadership as might be necessary. Yet, it is clear from official records that the Jedburghs were regarded as post D-Day reserves, something that those who would be recruited would perhaps not realise. The historian, M R D Foot, refers to the Jedburghs as a stiffening force, which seems apt, there to strengthen the incumbent Resistance forces.[26] The stage, as it were, was set for the idea to now develop more fully.

---

26 Foot, *SOE, The Special Operations Executive 1940-46*, London:BBC, 1985, p.127

Planning included determining the equipment the teams would need and SOE liaised with others including MT, ADL and the General Staff, it is noted in official records that this was an interesting case of co-operation between these groups. An exercise called 'Dachsund' was organised by the staff of stations IX and XII. Changes were made to the original equipment used in Spartan; this exercise also tested the idea of how well a team could demolish a bridge without advance reconnaissance. The question was could they simply turn up, adapt to the local situation and carry out the necessary sabotage; the answer, when in the field, would be a firm yes.

Meanwhile one day in Scarborough, a notice went up for volunteers for special duties. One of Fred's Bovington friends spotted the notice first and all four friends decided, in spite of the vagueness of the call to apply. Fred couldn't recall the notice clearly, but said he recalled something about parachutes and special duties. Stanley Cannicott, in the OTC (Officer Training Corps) at the time, recalled his poster, which said 'Volunteers who are interested in parachuting and guerrilla warfare and a knowledge of French, step forward.'[27] Fred, in some interviews, seemed to recall the Balkans being mentioned in his poster. Clearly for Fred and many others anywhere and anything would be better than where they were. This notice had been sent from the SOE with permission to various locations.

In October 1943 Fred and others were despatched for interviews and testing near Oxford. Fred recalled there were between forty and fifty Royal Armoured Corps radio operators at the interview centre. They were all given medicals and they were also interviewed by a psychiatrist. Fred recalls there was questioning about family and he sensed they wanted men without families. Additionally questions were on the war, his feelings about it, what fears he had and how he thought he might cope with stress. Fred said through the questioning he got an idea of what he might be getting himself into, but didn't fully appreciate the experience to come.

However, recruitment for the Jedburgh operation proved more of a challenge than initially anticipated; both the British and Americans needed the approval of the relevant authorities to recruit. In Britain that was the GHQ Home Forces and in the US the C G E Tousa ETOUSA (European theatre of operations). In September 1943 it had been decided to begin training the Jeds on 1 January 1944 and that they would be based in a single location. It would also be quite separate from any other SOE training centre, and rather than having the standard STS (Special

---

27 Stanley Cannicott, *The Journey of a Jed*, Cheddar: Cheddar Valley Press, 1986, courtesy Imperial War Museum

Training School) and number would be given a different identifier. This was done for security reasons only, this way any soldier captured would have little knowledge of any SOE training school or those within it. Milton Hall in Peterborough was chosen and was given the identifier ME65 and called the 'Allied Commando School'. While it was a joint British/American establishment, initially at least it was far more British than American. Nevertheless, not all training would be undertaken at Milton Hall and both the British and American Jedburghs would complete some training elsewhere before arriving at Milton Hall.

The SOE which had various departments for each country and for France there were eventually six sections, the main one being the F Section, with various other sections dealing with specific areas, for example RF which dealt with De Gaulle's Free French, the EU/P which dealt with the Polish in France, the DF which dealt with escape lines and from 1942 the AMF section from Algiers. Now there was a new section the DR/JED section, which would liaise with other departments of SOE for everything relating to the Jeds, from recruitment to pay, through equipment, organising plans and despatch of teams.

When it came to recruitment, officers were to be seen by the 205 selection board at Stodham Park, STS 3, at Liss in Hampshire.[28] The officers, British, French or the small number of Belgium or Dutch all had to pass the same assessment board.

Officers would be graded as to their suitability for the Jedburghs, there were four grades;

A- Outstanding
B- Good
C- Fair
D - Indifferent

No one with a D grade was accepted and the majority were ranked A or B.[29] When it came to American personnel the board was free to record honest opinions but could not fail them as they had already gone through their own recruitment process,[30] although there seems some anecdotal evidence suggesting some were replaced once in England.

During this period the Signals Section worked tirelessly and developed what came to be known as the 'Jed Set'. It had to be

---

28 There is now an information board adjacent to Liss Railway Station, detailing the wartime role the village played. It was placed by The Secret WW2 Learning Network
29 National Archives, HS7-17
30 Ibid

efficient, able to work without a separate power source and be practical enough to be carried. The set developed with a transmitter powered by a hand generator and a small receiver powered by battery, the overall weight allowing for one spare battery was 30lbs, any additional batteries weighed 3lbs. The range was 600 miles and the life of the battery was 60 hours. Codes for the radio operators were also developed at this time.[31]

The pay for the British Jeds was interesting as it was decided, for security reasons, they would receive their pay and allowances from army funds. Jeds from other nationalities would be paid by their respective countries. As time went on it was decided to pay the British Jeds an additional 5 shillings a day to bring them more into line with Jeds from overseas, such as the Americans who were paid more. It was realised that there needed to be pay parity.[32]

As well as attempting to equalise the pay, it was also decided that the British radio operators needed to hold the same rank as their American counterparts, so were raised to the rank of sergeant.

The SOE and SO department of the OSS compiled a report in December 1943 giving details of the plans and progress. By this review the team structure had once again changed, now it would be two officers and one national of the country. Rather than being dropped close to the front line they would be dropped further behind enemy lines to assist the resisters and provide vital radio communications. In essence their role was to utilise the full capability of the resistance forces of the country they dropped into, which would require tact and leadership as well as exceptional fighting skills. These were the criteria on which recruitment focused.

At recruitment the type of officer that was sought would possess the abilities somewhere between those of an agent and those of commando capable of fast and efficient strikes.[33] Official papers list six qualities required, however, it was expected that many of these skills would be developed during training so the recruiters were initially looking for men who had the following qualities:

1. Ability to mix well with others, particularly with other nationalities, and a general intelligent sympathy with the problems of other nations, with particular regard to the way these would affect the military situation.

---

31 Ibid
32 Ibid
33 Ibid

2. Ability to take a quick and intelligent grasp of any situation that might arise, and to make a decision as to the best course of action to pursue.
3. The ability to absorb information and learn what was required within a reasonably short period of training.
4. A1 physical fitness and ability to endure possibly extremely hard conditions, and the necessity for continual vigilance and frequent movement, probably mostly at night.
5. The ability to command and lead others and to pass on knowledge gained in training to those who might later come under his command.

These are the six skills required, many of which would be gained during training.

1. A good general knowledge of the history of the Resistance forces of the country to which he was being sent, and an interest in their potentialities and the best uses to which they could be put.
2. A solid groundwork of military training and tactics, involving the deployment of small numbers of men (equivalent to a company).
3. A good knowledge of small arms and the ability in the use and maintenance of rifle, Sten, pistol and certain Anti-tank weapons.
4. A general knowledge of explosives and their uses for demolition.
5. A working knowledge of the language of the country.
6. A working knowledge of wireless and of code and cypher.

The feeling was that most would be operating in France and it was decided that 60 British officers with 40 British radio operators would be required and that the Americans would provide the same numbers, France would provide 100 officers. Additionally, it was estimated that 6 Dutch and 6 Belgian officers would be required to drops in those countries. It was felt that there would be 75 teams for France with 6 each for Holland and Belgium. Up to 12 teams would be held as reserves, to allow for failures during training and casualties in the field.

Many of the British officers recruited were taken from SOE sources in the Middle East, originally trained to work in the Balkans but the changing political situation meant they were not required. Most of them were accepted on their return to England with other officers drawn from SOE training instructors and staff officers. Some were recruited following a circular issued by the War Office Personnel Branches, but they were a small number. The whole project was in jeopardy when the French were unable to supply a sufficient number of officers. By February 1944 Major Turquet along with a representative of the American OSS were despatched to North Africa and fortunately garnered a good number of well-trained officers.

When it came to Fred and the other radio operators, the aim was for 40 British, 40 American and just 12 French, the low number of French was due to the lack of appropriately trained personnel available.

All this planning had been going on while Fred and others were joining up, going through basic training and then being deployed to various regiments. For the British radio operators though, SOE would look primarily at those from the Royal Armoured Corps. The reasoning for this was that there was a pool of already well-trained radio operators with a good knowledge of Morse, so the presumption was that they would be up to a good standard which was being demanded by the Jedburgh section. The vast majority, 37 out of 43, of British Jedburgh radio operators came from the Royal Armoured Corps. Fred would only discover later that they had been particularly keen on tank radio operators.

For Fred and his three friends, they had, unsurprisingly, never heard of the SOE nor had any idea quite what they were getting themselves into. They passed the tests, although did not know that at the time. While there seemed to be a specific list of requirements for officers, the NCO radio operators seem to have been chosen based on their radio skills, physical fitness and their ability to pass the psychological tests. Fred seemed to find the testing fairly easy and relaxed in its approach.

American involvement

Simultaneously across the Atlantic, moves were afoot to recruit for the American contingent of the Jedburghs.

It seems the medical was more a test of ingenuity rather than medical fitness, reports of officers wearing sunglasses for their eye test while failing to mention they were prescription. At least one officer threw his medical in the bin, having failed and said he had lost it but was fit for duty. Jack Singlaub, who lived to 100 and died just a few short months before Fred, gave wonderfully colourful descriptions of his experiences.[34] It might seem to some that this disregard for rules was at odds with military men, but actually for the Jedburghs this was just the

---

34 Jack Singlaub, *Hazardous Duty*, New York: Summit Books, 1991

sort of man they needed. They had to be creative, be able to think on their feet and not simply follow orders. Many of the American recruits had shown in their pre-war lives a penchant for action; one had sailed around the world, another was a Hollywood stuntman.

The selection process for the officers involved them being billeted at a country club just outside Washington. While they weren't sure what was going to be asked of them, they all to a man no doubt enjoyed the surroundings of Area F as it was known.

In the United States, recruitment of the radio operators was also underway. For some, like Bob Kehoe, he had begun to feel a sense of futility, much like Fred. Ready and willing but apparently going nowhere fast. A secretive major talking about hazardous duty had piqued his interest, in much the same way the announcement on the wall had for Fred and his friends. A few weeks later he was on a train with a bunch of other radio operators heading for who knew what.[35]

Eventually the officers and radio operators all met up and for the first time got a proper hint of the work they would be involved in. Guerrilla warfare.

For the British recruits, they had been in the war for a few years, but for the Americans it was going to be a new experience and certainly for the officers, they needed to get up to a level that was equal to the British.

It must be remembered that at this point, it was the British who were the superior partner, the Americans had the men and the money but lacked experience.

The American radio operators reportedly had a very rough crossing over to England with injury and sickness befalling many. Without doubt some questioned their initial enthusiasm, youthful ignorance and a desire to be heroic was knocked out of many on that Atlantic crossing.

Having undergone training in the United States, many Americans believed they were ready for action and were frustrated to be placed in training. Maurice Buckmaster, head of the French section, is reported to have said to Herbert Brucker 'it would simply be murder to send you on an operation with just OSS training'. Brucker and his colleagues were not impressed but had to admit that the British training was far superior and Brucker said it made most of his OSS training seem amateurish.[36] It's noteworthy that of the 55 American officers sent from the United

---

35 Colin Beavan, *Operation Jedburgh*, New York: Penguin Books, 2014, p.70

36 Captain John Tyson in 1943, who said the American training was entirely inadequate. Charles Briscoe, Major Herbert Brucker, SF Pioneer, *Veritas* Vol. 3, No2, 2007

States, only 35 actually became Jedburghs. Additional Americans were recruited on the ground in Britain to rectify the shortfall.

Gearing up

Back in England, with Fred having been accepted for special operations, now the work began. In around October - dates are a little vague with Fred and others stating differing start times - Fred found himself and several friends moved to Henley on Thames. The radio operators were at Fawley Court, an SOE school, known as STS 54a, it was part of the SOE Signals Section. Fred talked of Countess Gardens where he was billeted while undergoing training at Fawley Court, a short distance away. This property was a Victorian building, today a listed building. They had very comfortable surroundings with first class food and Fred was one of around 50 men staying there, frankly it was luxurious compared to what some were facing. At Fawley Court, Fred and his fellow radio operators were put through their paces. For Fred and most of the British radio operators, having trained with the Royal Amoured Corps, their standard was reasonable, a normal army speed of between 10-12 words a minute but SOE demanded 25 words a minute so that they would have the ability to maintain a steady 20 words a minute out in the field. This requirement to improve to a higher level for SOE standards, meant that Fred and the others spent hour after hour working to improve speed and accuracy. However, every hour of morse was then followed by a short break outside. These short 15-minute breaks seem to have often turned into impromptu no-rules rugby, with everyone pitching in.[37] As time went on and speeds increased, Fred recalled there would often be someone missing who had not made the grade. For the very few who did not make the grade, it's unclear whether they simply returned to their units or it has been suggested that they moved to be base radio operators, purely from a security point of view. One suspects that those who dropped out early might have simply been returned to their units whereas those who underwent more training could not be returned to their units on security grounds. Harry Verlander mentions one chap who was sent packing but only because he had quite ingeniously found wine behind a wall at Fawley Court and gone off to sell it around Henley.[38]

As time went on those remaining moved on to learning 'Q codes'. These were international codes which allowed three letter messages to

---

37 Harry Verlander, *My War in SOE*, Bromley: Independent Books, 2010, p.48
38 Ibid, p.51

convey longer sentences, thereby shortening the time required to be on the radio. For example, 'QRK' meant 'Are you receiving me?' After these were mastered, it was time for coding and decoding messages. Cyphers were complex, obviously, and a fellow Londoner named Leo Marks, came along to Fawley Court to explain his ciphering. Like Fred he was a cockney so very popular with all the London men, was reputedly quite outspoken, swore like a trooper and explained that his very skilled staff were mainly female. However, he was keen that his system meant that a message never needed repeating, which was important for the safety of those in the field sending the messages. Fred said there were also various other speakers coming in, each one adding a little more to their understanding of what they would be doing. While there had been psychological testing at their initial selection, this did continue at Fawley Court, bespectacled men would come in for chats and to show inkblot pictures. This seems to have been taken in good humour and Fred said you simply said what you saw, or sometimes had a little fun with them, whatever that might have meant. Clearly the idea was to remove anyone who might not be up to the stressful requirements that the SOE demanded. Beyond improving their radio skills and having occasional fun with the 'trick cyclists' as the bespectacled men were known to Fred and others, there was a lot of physical training, with Fred mentioning a firing range in the basement where they could work on their small arms technique. Despite the intense nature of their time at Fawley Court, there was always a little time for fun. Fred was very discreet, not mentioning much about his social life during the war, but Harry Verlander, a friend of Fred's, was always more forthcoming. There were several pubs to frequent and given the frequent shortages, new drinks to try with beer sometimes missing, brandy, rum and other drinks were indulged in and for many tried for the first time. Fred's love of a gin and bitter lemon may well have been forged in the hostelries of Henley.

There were dances at the local dance hall, where young ladies were always happy to while away some time with a man in uniform and all the chaps seem to have attended at least occasionally. After around three months, training at Fawley Court was complete, the men who had come through the training were advised they were moving up to Sergeant - which apparently pleased them all very much, the extra pay was welcome and they were told they were moving on to another location for further training. Arthur Brown states that while at Fawley Court, both French and American radio operators arrived and slotted into the training. Nevertheless, they were apparently not aware that the reason for the rise in rank was in fact to bring them into line with the Americans who they would soon be working alongside and a 5 shilling a day 'special pay' would be added to bring them into line with others who were being paid that little bit more. This extra pay, unlike their regular pay, was not directly from army funds but from another unknown source; presumably SOE had its sources.

Dates throughout are a little vague but it would seem that it was around Christmas that the change in rank occurred. The festive celebrations seem to have been enjoyed, with memories of good food being recalled many years later. A few hardy individuals decided to take a festive swim in the Thames, but Fred was not one of them as far as we know. It certainly would have been out of character for him to dive into freezing water.

Officers for the Jeds were elsewhere, divided across two further schools with training at this level designed to last between six and eight weeks with a move to Milton Hall by the second week in February. While this plan seemed fair from a training point of view, it missed the fact that Milton Hall would not be ready. This made life difficult for all in the early weeks.

Milton Hall

Milton Hall was a manor house near Peterborough, north east of London. Many properties were requisitioned during the war and this was one such location. The rather elegant oak-panelled bedrooms were converted into dormitories, as well as there being huts close to the house for those not lucky enough to get a spot in the main house and all the men were assigned randomly, another way to ensure they mixed and got on.

In January 1944, after enjoying a short post festive leave, Milton Hall, also known as ME65, was the location that the Jedburghs came together properly. This was an entirely separate location to any other SOE training school, even in name; other sites were known under the code of STS with a number. This was to ensure a separation of the military Jeds from the rest of SOE, to maintain their military status, these were soldiers not spies. The first commandant at Milton Hall was an experienced traditional officer, Lieutenant Colonel F V Spooner, but his traditional approach did not work at all with this unique group.

A half-hearted attempt was made to get everyone on parade. It is fair to say that the British made a fair attempt, but the Americans ambled around with hands in pockets, ignoring any attempt to get into line and apparently muttering that they would only listen to American officers and the French simply didn't understand. After this all attempt at formal military behaviour was left at the gate, no saluting and certainly no attending for parade. These chaps, viewed as irregular by many who knew of their existence, were certainly showing that they had an independent streak that traditional regiments and units would not tolerate. Spooner was successfully replaced by Lieutenant Colonel Musgrave, again a British officer but one who understood that this group of men required a less traditional level of handling. His second in command was Major H W Fuller, who ultimately became part of a Jed team and was replaced by Major McLallen, who apparently possessed more tact than his predecessor and had the confidence of the students.

The American contingent had trained in both the US and in England, but now all the Jeds were gathered in one place. This obviously was for final training but also for the men to meet and organically form their teams. This organic mingling to assemble a team was common for aircrew in the RAF, and the Jeds were placed together to see how they got on with each other. From this the men got to know each other a bit, obviously there was some segregating on nationalities, but overall they all got on with the job they were there to do. Some seem to recall nominations for various teams, but official records show that the officers were allowed to request members for their teams. For some of the English the brash Americans were a little hard to take initially but things settled down and inevitably American often went with American and British with British. There is often a misconception that teams were made of one American, one British and one French, but more often than not there were two Americans or two British with one French. This made sense given the need for immediate and reactive decisions in the field and a need for ease of understanding, there was no room for colloquial misunderstandings.

The six-week training regime was, according to Fred, tough but fair with the time allocated as follows:

Unarmed Combat	12 Hours
Demolitions	39 Hours
Weapon Training	54 Hours
Map Reading	37 Hours
Fieldcraft	27 Hours
Minor Tactics	22 Hours
Appreciations and Orders	9 Hours
Reception Committee Work	10 Hours
Anti-Tank Mines	10 Hours
Recognition of Enemy units	10 Hours
Parachute Training	24 Hours

Signalling	18 Hours
First Aid	4 Hours
Physical Training	42 Hours
French	42 Hours
Indoor Exercise	42 Hours
Recreational Training	60 Hours

Each subject was then split down, for example map reading consisted of ten lectures with seven practical sessions and one session which combined both lecture and practical, the course finished with a written 4-hour test.[39] While French was on the curriculum, Fred said he had arrived with schoolboy French, but he found living alongside French officers and radio operators the best way to improve and he said that by the time he went into France, his French was good enough to carry him through. Indeed years later, he could switch quite easily into French if the need arose. There are some anecdotal reports that some Americans never quite got to grips with the French language.

Although he didn't know it at the time, for Fred the four hours of first aid training would prove invaluable when he reached the Far East with Force 136.

In addition to the training given by in-house trainers, external lecturers were brought in. Hugh Verity, perhaps one of the best known names gave a talk on Air Operations from the RAF angle. Flight Lieutenant Bartter is listed as giving a talk on Experiences on Operations, I believe this to be Peter Bartter, who flew with 138 Squadron, dropping agents and supplies into occupied territories. He had been shot down over Denmark, but had brought the aircraft down without mishap. Three of the officers had evaded and returned to England with the rest of the crew captured. He was teaching at the nearby STS 40 and his knowledge of transporting equipment and agents would have given the men a good understanding of what to expect.[40] Leo Marks, head of cypher at SOE, was another lecturer and one Fred along with the other radio operators would have remembered from Fawley Court and paid attention to.

One of the most interesting lectures for the men would have been given by 'Jerome', who was in fact G E Brault, a radio operator working in occupied France for Paul Schmidt. He had been captured,

---

39 National Archives, HS7-18
40 Nigel Atkins, Jan Christensen, *Secret Operations over Occupied Europe*, Barnsley: Airworld, 2024, p.134

with five cars arriving outside his lodging, while he was transmitting to London. He was able to get a message off and destroy the messages he was yet to send. Helped by a sympathetic guard he was able to escape. His lecture also showed a short film from France, which would have given the men a brief glimpse of a country most had never seen. Many would reflect that talks given, especially by agents, were sobering events.

Fred remembered Daphne Parks very well and her lectures on cyphers; he thought very highly of her. He said she didn't suffer fools and really knew her stuff. The Jeds were trained on 'one-time pads', which Fred thought were superb, unbreakable unless you were caught with it. It was a pad with random letters and numbers with base having the same pad in order to decode. There was further intensive training on Q codes with another example being 'QUG' which meant imminent danger and the operator was closing down. According to Arthur Brown an American succinctly rephrased to 'Guess who's here and with what?'

Across a few months and allowing for sleep, this was an intensive course.

While Fred and his colleagues had found the work at Fawley Court hard, now things stepped up even more. Jack Singlaub, an American Jed, stated that they would work for eleven days straight and then be allowed three days off. For the Americans, London seems to have been the preferred location for their time off. Yet, other British members state there was no time off and they could not leave Milton Hall.

Days began at six with some physical training, then breakfast, the day then unrolled with a mixture of training and lectures including language classes. Often finishing at nine at night, that only left an hour for any social chat before lights were out at ten.

The grounds of Milton Hall had been planned and arranged for final training, so as well as the obligatory assault courses, there were firing ranges, even a fuselage to practice jumping out of - into a sandpit. There were specific areas for explosives training including throwing hand grenades. There were also zones for armed and unarmed combat. Fred often referred to training in silent killing. These men were prepared and trained for pretty much any eventuality. Beyond this, survival training was also given to ensure that the men could survive in the countryside without provisions if necessary. Musgrave, who had hunted big game in Africa, gave many lectures and was popular with the men. On one day he took the men into he grounds and selected one of the sheep, a number of which roamed the grounds as natural lawn mowers. He then proceeded to slaughter and skin the animal to teach the men how to get food and even smoke it for later if needed. He stated it was vital that they could feed themselves and live off the land, should it be necessary. It seems Harry Verlander bagged the skin, got it cured and gave it to his mother to use as a bedroom mat for many years.[41] It now resides at Harrington Aviation Museum along with many other Jedburgh items. Beyond the sheep experience, training also included foraging for food. Instructions were given for preparing snakes to eat, it was simple, cut off the head, skin it and boil for 10 minutes. There were suggestions to use mice or rats with dandelion leaves to make a stew. This would be vital for some and less of an issue for others, but perhaps explains Fred's love of good food and wine in later life.

Both the radio operators and officers crossed over in terms of training. The radio operators were trained so that in an emergency they could take over from the officers. The officers also underwent some training in communications, so that again in the case of the death or incapacity of their radio operator they could handle the radio sets.

The Americans brought with them their PX (Post Exchange) supplies and these seem to have proved popular with all, perhaps because, as Harry Verlander commented, they were cheaper than the NAAFI (Navy, Army, Air Force Institues). It seems many were converted to smoking Camels or Chesterfields as well as the odd cigar. Fred certainly enjoyed a good cigar post-war and this, no doubt, is where he was first introduced to them. Fred seemed to find the rations more than agreeable, saying they were very well looked after and the American influence was appreciated by the other nationalities.

The arrival of the Americans brought a tradition to the Jeds, during one particularly boring lecture, some American called out 48, 49, 50 Some Shit or according to the CIA (Central Intelligence Agency) website, Bullshit - this became the cry of the Jeds whenever something was deemed a waste of time or simply boring. Fred was certainly a man who did not suffer fools and it would seem that this was a trait of the Jeds.

The issue was that there were multiple ranks and so many backgrounds, commandos, regular army and of course several nationalities, who all had their own ideas and beliefs as to how things should be done. This farrago of individuals who all had some special qualities to qualify for the Jeds meant that almost inevitably there was a risk to the strictures of military protocol. There was also the issue of how to pronounce Jedburgh, with the Americans saying Jedburgs, the French Geed-Bore and the British, Jedboro – this is perhaps why

---

41 Harry Verlander, *My War in SOE*, p. 55

they always referred to themselves as Jeds, they could at least agree on the first part of the name. Fred never seemed to care how it was pronounced, but did always use the shortened Jeds when speaking about this period of his life.

Unlike regular army regiments, the men had choices ranging from which firearm they favoured to which clothes they preferred. Most, including Fred, favoured the Colt. 45 as their personal weapon and took the British fighting knife. Clothing seems to have been equally mixed between British and American options - many chose the American boots but British woollen comforters and smocks.

What is clear is that this idea of a multi-national special force was so new that anything went. If the men didn't like the idea of something it was dropped, as in the saluting and going on parade. Many standard army rules were dispensed with, yet the men were military and had their training. They relied on the discipline which had already been instilled in them, but there was leeway.

This unusual way of running a unit, which had seen a change in leadership at Milton Hall fairly early on, clearly demonstrated some could not handle what some may have viewed as a lassez faire attitude. But that should not be mistaken for a lack of commitment or any failings in skills. These men were well trained, disciplined and prepared to be dropped behind enemy lines, so hard and fast rules were not going to work with them. They had to think on their feet, and would have to in order to survive, therefore, they were by their very nature, unlike regular soldiers, they were Baker Street Irregulars.

While at Milton Hall and before the end of the second month of training, the men were taken to Tatton Park and Ringway near Manchester for parachute training. They had a fuselage at Milton Hall, to practice jumping out of - but jumping into a sandpit was somewhat different to jumping from an aircraft.

The men travelled in groups to Tatton Park, which was a large estate, which included Ringway airfield. The estate was also used for evacuated children and the land was worked by the Land Army, which consisted mostly of women. In addition it had a starfish site from August 1941 until April 1943. These were decoy sites to draw enemy bombing away from urban areas. Fires would be lit during bombing raids to draw enemy bombers away from Manchester. Beyond this it was also home to No 1 Parachute Training School, according to Tatton Park records.[42] They note that 383,000 descents were made, by both

---

42 Tatton Park, The Estate at War, https://www.tattonpark.org.uk

military and civilians. SOE lists Ringway as STS51; there were three houses within the grounds used by the Jedburghs. These would have kept them separated from others completing training. Fred often spoke of those couple of days when they were sent to Ringway for their parachute training. For Fred the worst jump was from a balloon, six of them were winched up in a cage, a flight lieutenant as their instructor. Fred said the six of them were clinging to the side of the basket and there was just silence, none of them were feeling very confident. As they had been ascending in this cage, the instructor said to them that he had a 48-hour pass and he didn't want them messing about. Once up to the required height they were all given a fairly hefty shove out through the hole in the bottom of the basket, there was no time to worry. Once they were down, the instructor jumped, landed and hopped on his motorbike to disappear for his leave. Fred would roar with laughter recalling this event, the sight of the instructor disappearing and leaving them standing there. After this there were two other jumps, one in the daylight and one at night. Fred said the night jump was odd, there was no horizon to allow you to get your bearings, you jumped into nothing. This was abridged parachute training, covered in a couple of days.

Once parachute training was complete, the rest of the training intensified even more. The firing ranges were always busy, with training on drawing one's pistol fast and efficiently and from different stances, standing or crouching, the firing range has been described as akin to the wild west.

As time went on, further training away from Milton Hall began, for Fred this included going to Scotland to set up and radio back. They were transported to Dunbar and from there would practice sending messages back to base. Fred said they went up to Scotland in groups for two weeks at a time and that it gave them some sense and experience of what it might be like to be in the field and having to attempt to communicate important information back to base. Arthur Brown, a fellow radio operator, felt these were confidence-building exercises for the men and to help them get used to the equipment they would use once deployed. The irregular nature of their training meant that those in Dunbar for New Year 1943/44 enjoyed some high jinx which saw at least one of their party spending the night in the local police station. Apparently it caused quite a buzz and all were happy to return to Milton Hall. No-one seems to have recorded what these high jinx were and Fred certainly never admitted to anything. As well as trips to Dunbar, exercises were also carried out in Charnwood Forest in Leicestershire. These involved radio exercises and rehearsals of receiving orders and meeting up with 'resistance forces'.

Other exercises took the role of being dropped in the countryside and told to find their way back to Milton Hall - of course they had no papers or money and were told in no uncertain terms not be caught by the Home Guard or police. These excursions were fun for the most part, although a few came close to being caught, some allowed themselves to be caught once they had achieved their objective and some cheated by making sure they had some money in case food became available rather than having to kill and live off the land.

It seems they found the Home Guard keen and eager, so it was a fair test each time. One exercise involved breaking into an American Air Force base to plant fake explosives on the aircraft - it was a bit of a bust as the base had been forewarned. All exercises though were treated with the respect they deserved; the men were all aware that it would be their response and reaction to events which could determine their fate. It's fair to say though that some teams took whatever advantage they could. There is a rumour that one team hijacked a train to aid their return to Milton Hall on one exercise. Another team simply knocked on a farmhouse door asking to buy some food, only to find a hospitable farmer who fed them and gave them a comfortable bed for a night. These occasions though show that the men used their initiative and ingenuity and both of these skills would be required when they dropped into France. They accepted their training and worked hard to ensure they were ready and after three months of solid training were deemed ready.

Fred recalled one forced march in the Fens, marching along in the dead of night he said suddenly one of the Americans fell in a ditch at the side of the road. It turned out he had fallen asleep as he walked and toppled into the ditch. Such incidents were viewed with great amusement by all.

Solidifying this international group of men into one unit though was difficult and they needed a common bond as well as the common enemy they shared. A competition to design a Jedburgh badge was organised and Captain Victor Gough's entry was declared the winner. All would wear this badge with pride. The design and designation Special Force bound these men both during and after the war. Sadly, Captain Gough was murdered by the Gestapo, of his three man team only one survived, the French team member was killed in action, his British sergeant was captured yet very fortunately and likely unexpectedly survived the war. There is the suggestion that there were alternate options for the SF mark, Sans Femmes or Sexually Frustrated are the more lighthearted suggestions that appeared in an American hand out prepared by their reunion committee.[43]

---

43 Quoted on an American Military Forum, US Militaria Forum

After three solid months, finally they were allowed some leave. Most of the British headed into Peterborough. They found the town abuzz with American airmen and it's fair to say that the American and French were more popular with the local girls. Nonetheless, local dances were a place to enjoy some company if that's what they wanted or alternately a quiet evening in the pub was also on offer.

Fred was a man who never spoke much of any romantic dalliances during this period, but there's no doubt from his occasional comment or wry smile that he enjoyed the company of a young lady or two during this period. Others were a little more forthcoming and Harry Verlander was wonderfully indiscreet about his romantic dalliances and recalls them in detail in his book.

Sorting the men into final teams seems, from what Fred said, to have been a fairly straightforward process, as previously described. Others have commented that preferences were stated and nominations made. Fred said he was specifically asked by Captain Smallwood to join his team, which he was delighted about. He liked Smallwood, he was typical of the Jeds, didn't suffer fools and spoke plainly.

Over the course of training, once teams were set, they were graded with about 60% rated as first class, around 25% were viewed as having a good average performance with 15% coming in at a slightly less high standard. For those in the lower group they would not be allocated the most important tasks except in an emergency and were most likely held as reserves. The overall training had resulted in a group of highly trained individuals and even those in the lower group would still be well above the average soldier in terms of training and ability.

The Jeds were a completely new idea, international and secret, everyone involved was learning as they went and naturally there were bumps along the way. Yet, Fred never really commented on any of this, he always spoke positively and with very happy memories of his time training at Milton Hall. It was undeniably tough both physically and mentally at times but he and others bore it with good humour. While no doubt some rubbed others the wrong way, they were united in their aims and were fortunate to enjoy not just excellent training but good facilities and food at a time when those were not available to all. While some experienced frustrations during the training, Fred never suggested this, he was glad to be doing something with the promise of some action. The biggest problem to face both those training the Jeds and the Jeds themselves was, as mentioned, nationality and thereby cultural differences. Even then those from the same nation could have come from different sections of the service, some had little experience, yet others had seen combat. This ironing-out took time and some felt they were wasting their time. These were soldiers but they were quite a different breed to the military machine they had come from and this was actually what made them so good and so special. In order to iron out these differences and difficulties some reorganisation took place and those who were more experienced were given the opportunity to share their knowledge, which was good for all and relieved the frustrations that some felt. The training given was to the highest standard and every effort was made to anticipate and train the men for any eventuality.

But for all the training what would matter in the field would be the physical fitness and stamina of the men but equally important was their mental and moral fitness and indeed mental stamina.

Training had finished by May, in time for D-Day. Fred though was in one of the 15 teams chosen to go to Algeria, to deploy for the southern invasion. With Fred in one of the teams chosen for Algeria, the last day all the Jeds were together for want of a better phrase, a sports day was organised.[44] There were various athletic competitions and apparently general foolishness all round. Fred, his team and the rest of the teams chosen for Algeria set sail on the *Capetown Castle,* on 2 May 1944, a liner, like so many, requisitioned for the war effort. It took ten days for them to sail down to North Africa, for many including Fred this would be their first journey abroad.

---

44 Major Robert Gutjahr, *The Role of Jedburgh Teams in Market Garden,* Fort Levenworth: US Army and General Staff, 1978

CHAPTER THREE

FRANCE

The history of France during the Second World War has been covered innumerable times, the ignominy of invasion and occupation, the speed no one envisaged, the Maginot Line simply bypassed, along with a collaborating government remains a tender issue to this day. The extraordinary evacuation at Dunkirk may invoke ideas of patriotism with the multitude of boats rushing to the aid of the soldiers but it was a dangerous and difficult time for those in power. It would take years before an Allied return to France could be considered viable and the risk of an invasion onto British soil was a very real threat.

From the moment of occupation in June 1940 in France, resistance had begun, subtle acts of defiance growing over the years. The accidental bump which knocked over a drink, stomping feet in the cinemas during news reports. Even wearing the tricolour colours blue, red and white were all little acts of defiance, which could bring retribution.[45] De Gaulle, in his radio address on 18 June 1940 from London, used the word resistance, despite his own misgivings around using civilians. The idea was perhaps unintentionally formed. De Gaulle was, in fact, in this broadcast hoping to attract French from around the world to rally to free the homeland. Unfortunately, many simply did not want to and in France, rather than being a rallying cry, many didn't hear the broadcast at all. In fact, many would say that it was not De Gaulle who made them rise up, but their own determination to rid the country of the invader.[46] Yet organically a resistance was growing and while the idea of civilians running around with guns horrified De Gaulle, he came to realise there was true value in an armed resistance. He

---

45 Paul Simon, *One Enemy Only: The Invader*, London: Hodder & Stoughton, 1942, p.69
46 Julian Jackson, *France: The Dark Years, 1940-1944*, Oxford: Oxford University Press, 2001, p.386 quoting Henri Frenay, *La Nuit finira*

formed the BCRA and through the SOE deployed agents throughout France. There is no doubt that accepting and needing help from Britain was a challenge for him and one which post-war he attempted to minimise. The French were clear that they wanted the Germans out of their country but they did not want them replaced with a British/American occupation, albeit a friendly one. Misunderstandings and disagreements would often hamper efforts during the war years and would seep into post war relations.

From the earliest days there were moves for a more formal Resistance, underground newspapers were produced and groups coalesced to carry out more defined and damaging Resistance and sabotage. There were many, however, who were prepared to endure the occupation, and in many aspects life appeared to continue as before, but the creeping controls, the occupiers having access to more food and those that disappeared never to be seen again all contributed to a growing resentment. Additionally, while they were resisting the occupier there were differing aims and politics at play. Communist groups, while very effective, were viewed with suspicion by other groups, and there were anarchists, many who had fought in the Spanish Civil War, who now found a new cause in France.

Jean Moulin is perhaps the name that resonates most for people when thinking about the Resistance. Elected the youngest prefect in France, he was the link between local and national government in Chartres. When France fell he vowed to fight the invaders. In spite of capture which reportedly resulted in an attempted suicide, he managed to get to London and met with De Gaulle. He impressed De Gaulle and set about trying to organise the resistance into a more regulated and cohesive unit. Sadly, Moulin was captured during a visit to Caluire along with several Resistance leaders, he was tortured by the infamous Klaus Barbie in Lyon and died while en route to Paris. De Gaulle would declare him a great man and he was ultimately laid to rest at the Pantheon in Paris.[47]

The Allies' success in North Africa led to the shattering of any illusion that even part of France was free as the Germans occupied the rest of the country. France is a huge country though and it was simply not possible for the occupiers to control every corner of the country. This allowed for some development of the Resistance while also offering an escape for many caught up in the *Service du Travail Obligatoire*. In September 1942 the compulsory work service or *Service*

---

47 Christensen and Atkins, *Secret Operations over Occupied Europe*, p.42

du Travail Obligatoire (*STO*) law required men aged 18-50 and women aged 25-35 to register so that they could be transported to Germany for work. Early 1943 saw this law used to demand 250,000 workers, this further advanced the Resistance with hundreds if not thousands melting into the countryside to avoid working for the Germans and in time many took up arms to fight.[48] Any pretence of a benevolent occupier had long faded, executions country wide combined with the STO and by the autumn, Hitler's final solution for the Jewish question - *Endlösung Der Judenfrage* - was extended to France.

While many had been working on the idea of using the Resistance in the occupied countries for some time, the reality of harnessing these forces was far harder to realise.

As the Resistance continued to grow, both in numbers and effectiveness they were supported by either the F section or the BCRA, via the RF section. This support took the form of agents on the ground as well as equipment and supplies dropped in. The realisation within the Allies that these groups would need additional support when the time came to invade aided the argument for the Jedburghs.

When thinking about those who fought in the Resistance, the words of Monénembu in his fictionalised story of the French Resistance, *The Black Terrorist*, 'They were not heroes, Mister, they were simply desperate!' are worth recalling.[49] The resisters were, in normal times, just ordinary civilians for the most part; while there were some former French Army members, most were local people who wanted their country and their freedom back. They were just like the young men of the Jedburghs, wanting to defeat the enemy and regain freedom.

By 1944, the tide was turning and those under occupation could see light at the end of what had been a very dark tunnel. Eisenhower was placed in charge of SHAEF (Supreme Headquarters Allied Expeditionary Forces) and understood the importance the Resistance could play in aiding the Allies. If those on the ground could disrupt German troop movements, possibly stop them, then the planned allied invasion would stand a chance of success. Beyond this, Eisenhower needed the Resistance to step up as the Allies advanced and provide some form of government in the areas being released from occupation. The men and women of the Resistance were local and could, it was hoped, ensure an orderly transition back to the French.

---

48 Jackson, *France*, p. 228
49 Tierno Monénembo, *The Black Terrorist*, United States, Diasporic Africa Press, 2012, p.101

Finally the time had come for the Jeds to be called to action. A paper within official files lists tasks for the Jedburghs and gives a framework for what was expected of them.[50]

A - To Hinder the Enemy

1.
   a. Removal of or interference with road signs
   b. Destruction of petrol pumps
   c. Laying of tyre bursters camouflaged as small stones or hidden in dung
   d. Sniping at drivers at long range.
   e. Felling of trees across roads
   f. Erection of unguarded road obstacles and fire from unguarded pillboxes
   g. Interference with water supplies
   h. Opening and jamming of swing bridges
   i. Interference with electrical supplies by attacks on transformers, switching gear and pylons.
   j. Interference with gas supply
   k. Opening of flood gates, dams etc.
   l. Demolition of bridges which are already prepared so long as it does not interfere with the advance of Monénembo, Tierno. *The* troops.

2.
   a. Attacks on Locos (railways)
   b. De-railing charges
   c. Interference with railway signals

3.
   a. Attacks on aircraft - this would have been while they were on the ground
   b. Attacks on supplies
   c. Attacks on pilots when off duty

4.
   a. Cutting signal lines and removing large sections
   b. Secret cuts in communication lines - making it harder to locate and fix

---

50 National Archives, HS7

c. Cutting and incorrectly joining cables - again to disrupt and delay repair
   d. Felling of telephone poles across roads
   e. Laying tight wires across roads at neck height to disable enemy
   f. Using a silent Sten gun for sniper operations

5.
   a. Ambush enemy staff cars
   b. Silent killing of unaccompanied staff officers
   c. Attacks on enemy headquarters especially smaller ones

6.
   a. Attacks on enemy workshops to interfere with transport
   b. Remove tools from civilian garages making it more difficult for the enemy to repair damage to vehicles
   c. Destruction of enemy reserve vehicles

7.
   a. Destruction of Bomb and Shell Dumps
   b. Destruction of rations by fire or other methods
   c. Steal rations from the enemy.

Yet the first line of Benjamin Jones' doctoral thesis states, 'there is more to war than fighting'.[51] This is a very relevant statement when discussing the Jedburghs, each team could certainly be an effective fighting force, if required, but their role was so much more than that. They were there to ensure a unity of the Resistance and to provide leadership if it was needed and to train these civilians to fight and importantly to be able to strike and melt away.

The Jeds, having been trained and primed for action, were finally sent in to Northern France during the D-Day period. They would be under the command of Special Force Headquarters and were assured there were liaisons from Special Forces in place. All teams would carry a substantial amount of cash on them, both to buy items such as vehicles but to provide the Resistance with funds to enable them to function as needed. In addition they carried authorisation and an explanation of who they were and what they were tasked to do. Fred's card is shown in fig. 6.

---

51 Benjamin Jones, *Freeing France: The Allies, the Resistance, and the Jedburghs*, 2008, PhD, University of Kansas

What is perhaps not always appreciated is that the success of D-Day was not guaranteed. The Allies knew they would be in significant trouble if the Germans were able to move more divisions into the region. The way to maximise the potential for success was multi faceted. A fake operation to lure the Germans into thinking that any invasion would come closer to the Calais region ensured that the Germans kept significant forces in that area. Additionally specifically targeted bombing of transport links ensured disruption of men and supplies to the region. Finally it was an accepted fact that the Resistance would be vital in delaying at the very least or stopping any German advance. The troops landing would need time to get ashore, assemble and prepare any forward movement. It was this third factor and the need to coordinate and organise the Resistance that the Jeds were to be a vital force.

When it came to the plans for the Jeds' deployment, Overlord was naturally the primary action. Teams would be deployed with the aim of impeding movements of the enemy to the front line, disrupting communications and ensuring the Resistance were enough of a problem to compel the enemy to maintain forces away from the front line in order to deal with them. They were also to ensure the Resistance could provide some adequate form of government as areas were liberated, to ensure a smooth return to French governance.

There were very clear instructions on targets that the Jeds could not engage with, they were industrial targets, utilities except where used for military purposes, shipping, demolishing major bridges and no lasting damage to railway rolling stock or engines.

While this work is focused on Fred and his story, it would be wrong to ignore the wider story of the Jedburghs. The following is a very brief overview of the teams dropped in to the north of France. Fred and his friends and comrades were sitting in Algiers eagerly awaiting their orders to go in while the friends left behind at Milton Hall found themselves despatched to either Harrington Airfield in Northamptonshire or Fairford in Gloucestershire for their departure into France.

A significant number of teams, 10, were dropped to Brittany. The aim was to delay troop movements north to the beaches and later on to assist the allies in their advance. Other tasks included delaying the movement of the enemy from other areas of France, to stop them or at least delay them from heading north as reinforcements.

The resistance would be vital in railway sabotage which would delay large scale troop movements. There were various factions within the Resistance, the main ones being the FFI (Forces Françaises de l'Interieur, French Forces of the Interior) and the FTP (Franc-Tireurs et Partisans), this second one being communist. Both of these were supplied and dealt with by the British; De Gaulle's BCRA only dealt with the FFI. The issue for the Jeds was that the Special Air Service (SAS) was also in situ, while in Brittany some Jeds were attached to the SAS bases in order to stir up the Resistance and this proved effective. The SAS were a strike force, whereas the Jeds were a more subtle but equally deadly force. Additionally, the involvement of the SAS in areas where the Jeds operated did on occasion cause issues. While all were on the same side, tactics varied and the Jeds were disadvantaged on occasion when the SAS operated in close proximity, often disrupting the work of the resisters and thereby disrupting the work of the Jeds. The main issue for these problems was that the SAS had little knowledge of the Resistance or the Jedburghs, had they been appropriately prepared, they could have, in odd cases, aided rather than hampered operations. Team George though state that the SAS worked wonderfully with them, after a bumpy start.[52] It is suggested in official documents that the Jeds should have been in first, laying the groundwork and the SAS brought in when the time was ripe for open aggression. Instead in several instances Jeds and SAS went in alongside each other.

While Northern France and D-Day were the priority, orders were clear that the aim was to cultivate resistance around the northern coast and into Brittany. The Jeds would prove useful, garnering a very reasonable outcome which was effective towards the enemy. The resistance with support from Jeds plus the effective use of SAS teams allowed for support of the incoming troops on the northern beaches. Jedburgh teams offered support to SAS groups, for example SAS Wash was reinforced and supported by Jed team Frederick. When attacked the SAS team dispersed, melting away as was their directive, but Frederick was able to stay in the area and re-establish contact with the various resistance groups.

In Britanny, the Resistance aided by the Jedburghs and indeed the SAS groups made a real difference, while these actions can never be calculated estimates in official documents suggest they saved one division being deployed. This was an enormous saving of manpower and lives. In the north, many teams made valuable contributions with their core aims of providing leadership, as well as organisation, providing arms and of course communications. Beyond either attacking garrisons or protecting vital bridges, the Jeds supervised hospital set-ups and carried out mopping up of enemy personnel as the allied advance rolled on. These actions ensured that the Third US Army was able to take its main forces east and the enemy found itself in a pincer grip with the Allies advancing.

---

52 Team George, National Archives HS6-511

Team Giles consisted of a French Captain Lebel, an American Captain Knox and a British radio operator, Gordon Tack.[53] They enjoyed an excellent drop into their area of Finisterre in the most westerly part of Brittany on the night of 8 July 1944. Little was known of any Resistance in this area, so General Koenig had met with Captain Lebel prior to departure to emphasise the need for information. Greeted by an enthusiastic group of young men, who all needed a kiss from their new Allied friends, the group realised there were cars and a truck. They had been gearing up for a long walk, but instead packed themselves and their equipment into the truck. They were advised that due to the capture and execution of 12 of the Resistance leaders the previous week, things were a little disorganised locally. They travelled towards Chateauneuf du Faou to meet with the head of a local Maquis group. The last part of their journey in what was apparently a very loud truck was completed in broad daylight. They arrived a few kilometres from Laz, and found a fairly well organised group of about 50 living in the woods. Their chief was not there, so the team filled their time handing out arms and ensuring the men knew how to use them. The team then heard a message on the BBC and while worried returned to their drop zone to receive more supplies, this was a substantial drop, which they were still loading onto the truck in daylight. They made it safely back to their base, whereupon they heard that 300 German paratroopers had gone through Laz, searching all the farms. During the course of the day the team armed another group of maquis to the east of Laz and, in spite of the number of enemy paratroopers, the team remained safe.

As well as arming and training men, the team met with senior Resistance figures in the area and finally managed to persuade them to wait for orders from the Allies before commencing any action. This was not easy, these people suddenly well armed wanted to take the fight to the Germans and the Jeds were in place to ensure that everyone held back until the allies were ready to follow through. Beyond this the team organised medical services throughout the area, which ultimately saved countless lives. They organised the transport for other teams landing and organised multiple drop zones and reception committees for the said drop zones.

The team and the Maquis they were with were hunted by the Germans and had to move, walking through the night and through potentially dangerous areas and towns, having to move several times. Finally on 2 August, the radio beamed out the message they wanted to

---

53 National Archives, HS6-515

hear; armed conflict could begin. Unfortunately, for whatever reasons, the advancing Americans were not aware of the Jeds and did not make contact to determine the location of Germans. Had they done so, many lives including those of many innocent French civilians could have been saved. The American main column was ambushed and many French were killed by Germans in response to the advancing Americans. There was frustration from the team, they had communication contact through a Special Forces detachment at each Army headquarters. The ambush and the subsequent German reprisals against civilians could have been avoided by simple contact. Sadly, miscommunication or simply a lack of it would be a recurring theme for the Jedburghs.

As well as issues once on the ground, problems were sadly frequent when teams were dropping in. For Harry Verlander and Team Harold, the navigator made an error and they were dropped roughly 20 miles from where they expected to be.[54] Harry landed in a field, but had been taken aback to see houses and a village as he drifted down. The team were all safe but equipment was lost as parachutes failed to open and also what did land was spread around the village. This team were lucky to land in such a potentially exposed area and get away.

One team, Aubry, found themselves on the outskirts of southeastern Paris, they instructed a resistance group in sabotage and worked to ensure the railway was disrupted on a nightly basis.[55] They were in such a controlled area that they wore civilian clothing. Nonetheless, this close-quarters work resulted in the Resistance group being dispersed and the French member of Aubry being killed. It was not usual for Jeds to wear civilian clothing but in areas that were particularly active it was sometimes necessary. Team Alfred was one which seems to have been more fortunate, they worked clandestinely in civilian clothing and were ultimately asked to protect the bridges over the Oise River.[56]

The Jed team Augustus was completely wiped out, having dropped just a day after Fred and team Citroen further south.[57] They dropped in the north, but having made contact with allied troops attempted to recross lines in order to carry on harassing the German rear line and ran straight into a German checkpoint during a dark and rainy night. They knew their papers would get them through but an inquisitive soldier

---

54 Team Harold HS6-521
55 Team Aubry HS6-483
56 Team Alfred HS6-475
57 Team Augustus HS6-484

started poking around the cart they were riding in, which under the hay were stacked a reasonable amount of arms and ammunition. All were shot as they fled.

Far more teams were despatched from England than Algiers, with most departing from either Harrington in Northamptonshire, fairly close to Milton Hall, or Fairford Airfield in Gloucestershire, which would have involved a longer journey. Some teams, it seems went to London for briefings. Some teams give fuller details on the immediate time before their departure, while others simply state the date they went in.

FRED IN SOUTHERN FRANCE

So much attention is often directed towards D-Day in the Second World War, the audacious invasion of Northern France, which signalled for so many the beginning of the end of the Second World War. Yet less seems to be told of Operation Dragoon, sometimes referred to as the second D-Day landing, in the south of France. Perhaps because it followed a few months after the Normandy landings and maybe because it was led by the American Army. But its significance should not be underrated.

As in the North of France, the armies of the allies advanced but ahead of them, behind enemy lines were those British, French and Americans with the Resistance, aiding the advance of their comrades. The Jeds' primary role in the south was to prevent movement of troops. Teams were tasked with ensuring the Pyrenees were not an easy escape route for the enemy troops with several teams tasked with the western area.

The campaign of August 1944, Operation Dragoon, spearheaded by the Americans, is relevant to Fred's story, for he and his team along with other Jed teams had hung around waiting for this.

Naturally, there were delays, the British were focused and interested in Northern France, they were not convinced by the need for a southern invasion. But as Alan Wilt said in his book, *The French Riviera Campaign of August 1944*, it had everything, friction between British and United States leaders, colourful commanders and a huge amphibious landing.[58]

The Jedburgh teams in the south were instrumental in interfering with communications, ensuring both reinforcements and evacuations of troops was disrupted. Several teams flanked the army's move north

---

58 Alan Wilt, *The French Riviera Campaign of August 1944*, Carbondale: Southern Illinois University Press, 1981

towards Grenoble along with the Resistance teams in that area. The teams assisted in liberating areas where Allied troops did not get to. They helped ensure the escape route to Spain was closed to enemy troops. Fred and Team Citroen were one of several who were effective in harassing the enemy with Fred mentioned in despatches for calling in an airstrike on a bridge to prevent an enemy column moving north.

In the south the estimate of the effectiveness of the Resistance was that it was equivalent to four or even five divisions. The Jeds had aided this and however relatively short their contribution was they were effective.

One aspect of the Jeds' work was to ensure that the Resistance did not rise up until the main forces were ready. It would have jeopardised lives and effectiveness for groups to activate before the arrival and therefore support of Allied troops. The Jeds had to keep the resistance ready and primed but hold them back from their obvious enthusiasm to wreak havoc. In spite of the occasional incident of independent thinking during training the Jeds were first and foremost army men and they worked to ensure those they were embedded with held fire until the right moment. Nonetheless, they did not have to hold the Resistance back for long.

Well for Fred, his team and others sent to Algiers, the invasion and their deployment just days before Operation Dragoon, was a very long time coming. They had been in Algiers for months, training, running exercises and of course enjoying the locality and its pleasures.

For Fred and Team Citroen, they were one of 25 teams despatched to Algiers, ready to head into Southern France in support of the upcoming Operation Dragoon. The first 15 teams, of which Team Citroen was one, were despatched to Algiers in May with a further 10 following later in June. Based at Camp W, a former French Army Cavalry Officer School, just outside Algiers, called El Riath. Fred remembered the large house was surrounded by greengage groves and orchards of nectarines and pomegranates, it must have all seemed very exotic to these young men. There was ongoing training, in the mountains outside Algiers and then they were ready and certainly by this time primed for action. Delays ensued for a few months, rather than going in at the same time as the northern assault they were held back, politics held them back rather than any military reasoning. Further delays including a fever which ripped through the radio operators, reaching a peak in July. The cause of the fever which was unknown, with medics calling it NYD (not yet diagnosed), this delayed and disrupted the deployment of the teams further. This fever had also impacted two men already deployed in the field. Captain

Austin of Team Ammonia became very ill and had to be withdrawn from the field. Arthur Brown of team Quinine also fell ill, recalling, in his own words, 'the punishing stomach aches and raging fever'.

Team Citroen consisted of Fred as radio operator, Captain John Smallwood and the French member of the team was Captain R Alcee, although his real name was Pierre Bloch. Their code names were Retif (Fred), Anne (Smallwood) and Laurent (Alcee).

Captain Smallwood seems to have been something of a non-comformist, no doubt perfect for the Jeds. In his Imperial War Museum interview he makes clear his disdain for his assessors at SOE and downplays his experiences even more than Fred did. He was clearly a no-nonsense man and that would have appealed to Fred, being almost dismissive of his contribution. It's almost laughable to hear him discuss his army career prior to the Jedburghs, suffice to say there was no love lost on his or the army's part.

Finally in August, those months of kicking their heels in Algiers were over and they were heading to France and the unknown. Their final training completed, which apparently included a 104-kilometre hike in the mountains during the Algerian summer. Their official file states their mission was to stimulate and sustain guerrilla warfare in the area, a fairly broad mission as was necessary, it allowed flexibility. They were, like all Jeds, offered the L tablet, a hard capsule containing cyanide, that if bitten down on would kill within seconds. Fred, along with a good many, if not all Jeds, refused to take it with him. He always said he didn't want to consider what might happen but knew he would fight to the death if he had to. Jack Singlaub recalled refusing his tablet, following a briefing by William Casey, who made it clear that there were orders circulated by the Germans in France to shoot them on sight.[59] His response, like Fred's, was that he wouldn't allow himself to be captured.

Unlike some Jed teams Team Citroen had no SAS base near them and were being dropped to the Perpendicular circuit.

Just as the Jeds in the north were aiming to stop the Germans, so those in the south needed to slow or stop the Germans heading north to reinforce their weakening position.

But the Jeds had to do so much more than that. They had to negotiate with the Resistance, smooth various factions, control those fighters who were perhaps understandably a little enthusiastic. There needed

---

59 Jack Singlaub, *Hazardous Duty*, New York: Summit Books, 1991, p.42

to be organisation and control in disrupting the Germans yet holding the Resistance back until the allies were ready to follow through.

Team Citroen left Algiers during the night on the evening of 13 August 1944. They were to be dropped approximately 50 kilometres north of Apt in the area of La Garde. The following is based on the official team report, interviews with both Fred and Captain Smallwood as well as Fred's personal recollections to family.

Captain Smallwood in his report, states that their objective was the usual Jed one, which makes it seem like a regular occurrence. He lists their objectives as to paralyse enemy movements, sabotage telecommunications and guerrilla warfare.

They left Blida on board an American Liberator at 19.00 and arrived over their drop zone at 00.30; the flight itself was uneventful with no flak. There were, however, issues with both the static line and the drop.

According to Fred, the flight crew were on their last operation, he said there was no flak as they crossed into France, but the crew were particularly worried, superstitious on their last sortie. While there appear to have been two dropzones, Captain Smallwood got permission from the American Colonel commanding the airfield to be dropped in the Vaucluse which was to be their area anyway. They were dropped in the correct location, around 50 kilometres north of Apt, where the reception committee was expecting equipment, not men. It seems the drop zone had been deemed only suitable for equipment, not personnel. The team was due to be dropped from 800 feet but the Liberator crew, would not risk flying low to drop them, but didn't tell the team that. Instead of a smooth exit at 800 feet a shambolic despatch from the aircraft took place at around 1800 feet, Captain Smallwood in his report does not hold back on their despatch from the aircraft. He states the flight was uneventful, taking around three and a half hours from Blida to the drop zone. The problems then began, only one safety pin for the static line, this resulted in both the B2 set and Fred's kit being smashed, Fred said it was a mangled mess of metal but that he still carried it. The aircraft did not throttle down for the despatch of equipment or men. Captain Smallwood was shoved out of the hole without ceremony but managed a fair exit, Alcee was not so fortunate, being shoved across the hole and hitting the other side before his exit. Fred wasn't given the opportunity to get his feet in the hole before he was bundled out of the aircraft. Smallwood is clear that they were not hesitating and recorded his displeasure. Notwithstanding this graceless exit from the aircraft, there is no doubt Team Citroen was delighted to finally be heading into action. Fred when recalling his drop into France always said he thought the ground was never going to appear. He said it felt like an eternity and he noted that had the Germans been in the area, they would have been picked off easily, before their feet would have had the opportunity to hit the ground. Having a bad despatch which was across the lights, when he finally hit the ground Fred was not in his ideal location, having landed in the middle of a brick works with piles of bricks all around him. Fortunately, he was not injured but as he often said he could easily have broken his back had he landed just feet in any other direction, but what equipment landed, which had also been despatched across the lights, was spread over 500 metres from the drop zone. All in all it had been a rubbish departure from the aircraft which the team were lucky to survive. Team Cinnamon, whose details are later in this chapter, dropped on the same evening but were not so fortunate. Captain Harcourt broke both legs on landing, again the drop was too high, too fast and ill timed which meant months of training were wasted for him. He did not disguise his fury in his report, calling it a deplorable accident with his whole team landing off target in woods, they were fortunate not to suffer more injuries and lose more equipment, their B2 set was also damaged. There were Jeds on other teams who did not survive the drop, one was a friend of Fred's, he and his team would locate the site of the grave of this Jed so that they could convey the news to the chap's family. Clearly there were lessons to be learnt by some air crews, special operations required a standard which the British had achieved over the war years with 138 and 161 Squadrons who could ably fly at low altitudes to safely deliver personnel and equipment safely. In these busy months of the European war and with demand so high, any crew was used for the Jeds and it is clear that this cost some dearly. It was also an economic loss, months of training for those killed or injured on despatch as well as equipment destroyed, it is easy to look back with a fury but it's also necessary to recognise just how pressured the situation was and how relatively few special duties crews there were.

Almost immediately that Fred landed, in the brickworks, he saw a man running toward him, a local who was delighted to see him. He kissed Fred on both cheeks, a new experience for Fred, and proceeded to thank him. Fred, so young, was initially overwhelmed both by the greeting and the pungent aroma of garlic from his new friend. Fred like most of his generation had little experience of such exotic ingredients like garlic and it was a memory which stayed with Fred throughout his life. It was this part of the landing that Fred would prefer to recall and laugh as he told the story of this chap running towards him. It was clearly a preferable point to focus on rather than the nature of the drop.

As well as losing his B2 set and his own kit being a mangled mess, the team discovered their container of Verey pistols was missing but they did have Team Cinnamon's. In time they were able to confirm that Team Cinnamon did not get any pistols but did have their ammunition so the location of their container remained a mystery. This was another area for complaint against the wider planning and organisation for the Jedburghs. Fred commenting on his kit being a mess, underplays the issue. The men had a pack of 34 pounds in weight, which they could increase with personal items up to 40 pounds. Mistakes happened which caused issues in the field for many teams. But these problems could cause obvious issues both in terms of life and death but also in gaining respect from the Resistance groups.

Once over the initial shock of landing, Fred was able to locate the rest of his team and they made contact with the local forces. They had not been expected at the drop zone, even away from Fred's landing place it was very rocky and not conducive to a landing of personnel. Nonetheless, Archiduc, real name Camille Rayon, met them and they moved swiftly from the drop site.

The following is taken from the team report with added information from Fred and Captain Smallwood's interview.[60] That same night the team met with Colonel Jean Constans, known as Saint Sauveur and Colonel Guillaume Widmer known as Cloitre in the field. They had a headquarters set up with Rayon. On the 15th the team made contact with Commandant Beyne, at his headquarters in Sault. There they met a Canadian Major Labelle, with the nom de guerre Paul, of mission Nartex, but he was both disinterested and unhelpful having no knowledge of the Jeds. What the team discovered was that Beyne's maquis were both well trained and well equipped with French officers in place. The problem was that they were very defensive, understandably, as they had only recently been heavily engaged with the Germans, which had disrupted their organisation. They were, nevertheless, more than willing to fight if the Germans came looking for them. Nonetheless they had no interest in looking for trouble, yet engaged in patrols, placing barrages on roads and continued to engage in small actions. Because of this and as the Maquis were reasonably well organised and equipped, the team decided to move on, slightly south, towards the Luberon mountains, which was where their targets were mainly based.

---

60 Team Citroen report, HS6-497, pers. Comms and IWM interview with Captain Smallwood

Due to difficulties with transport, it took Beyne until the 19th to source a suitable vehicle for the team. According to Fred it was a clapped-out Citroën which they were not convinced would take them very far. Fred recalled having to get out of the car and stand on the bumper in order to balance it and get all four wheels on the ground. As well as this questionable transport Beyne had provided two companies of Corps Francs to them, who would prove very useful. One of these companies was very experienced in demolitions and led by a man known as Paulo. They arrived the same day without incident in the area of La Bastide des Jordains, south east of Apt. Throughout their journey the team had stopped in small towns to organise defences and gave orders for various possible eventualities. This group led by allied personnel would have been a very welcome sight and given real encouragement to people that finally the end of the war for them was nearing. The following day, the 20th, the team moved slightly further south to Pertuis which they made their base. This was an active area for Resistance and the location that René Char had been based, the famed French poet, who after the war would associate with Picasso and Camus. He wrote candidly during his time in the Resistance and *Feuillets d'Hypnos* was acclaimed when published after the war. Char had been called to Algiers in July 1944, it's unclear whether Fred and the team met him at any point, but he had hidden his notebook in a building used by the Maquis so the team may well have been within feet of what would become a famed and important work. Pertuis had suffered loss during the war, one of those killed was Roger Bernard, a young man from the town, who unwittingly walked into the town of Céreste not realising it had been taken by the enemy. He was reportedly carrying a pistol and wearing American shoes; he was shot. This highlights the dangers those who joined the Maquis faced daily; while the Germans could not be everywhere in the South, it also meant they could turn up anywhere. Fred always said the Resistance in Pertuis were delighted to welcome them and accept any and all assistance.

This was the same day, the 20th, as the Americans arrived. It had been expected that the Germans would hold the Durance river but the Americans had been able to cross it. The team sent guides to meet the Americans, but this swift arrival meant the team had to adjust their plans. Nonetheless the arrival of the Americans did not mean all was over and quiet. On that day Smallwood and Alcee, with the bridge at Pertuis across the Durance demolished, went to see what the situation was. The two members of the team had taken the two Corps Franc groups with them but saw nothing. They decided to show themselves and shot a few rounds. It turned out there were some well camouflaged

Germans across the river who engaged with machine guns. The Corps Francs engaged the Germans for the rest of the day and did suffer one wounded. Captain Smallwood discussed the fast moving situation with the American Colonel and provided information, transport and interpreters. By use of the telephone, minute by minute information on German movements was provided, yet the American was only interested in defensive behaviour and not particularly interested in advancing north. After a few days the team met another American officer, far more engaged in advancing. He joined the team on a reconnaissance and due to what he witnessed, the Americans were able to advance 20 kilometres the very next day.

Smallwood noted that the area where they were was not best suited to the Maquis as there was little water in the countryside so the Resistance were situated in towns and villages. Their official report also states that it would have been useful to have some instruction on German vehicles as transport was poor in their area, yet vehicles left behind by the retreating forces were often useless as they had no knowledge of the mechanics. Fred obviously had to keep moving but said they often had warning of incoming German patrols so he had time to decamp and move on. The Germans would attempt to home in on radio signals, so swift, accurate messaging was vital and Fred's intensive training ensured he was more than capable. As the radio operator he was more protected than other members of the team, remaining hidden so that messages could be sent usually twice a day and received, although he did go on patrols and recces as required. As time went on Fred was able to gather much useful intelligence and pass it back to Algiers, yet it was not always accurate. The pace of the advance meant that situations changed rapidly.

Fred was fond of telling one story in particular and so it seems was Captain Smallwood. Fred recalled one of these days very clearly, they had loaded into a bus packed with explosives in search of the enemy, they were heading to a town to check on information that German tanks were there. On the road between Ansouis and Villelaure Fred recalled turning a corner and being faced by a single German tank. He roared with laughter as he described the mass bundle from the bus, everyone diving for cover lest the German fire and ignite the explosives. Everyone, that is except for one young man, who had only gone along as he wanted a new pair of boots from the next town. He grabbed a Mills grenade and climbed aboard the tank, thrusting the grenade through the drivers visor. Fred always said it was the bravest thing he saw, it certainly saved lives. There were casualties from this event, one French Resistance fighter being killed. Although Fred said it was a solitary tank, official reports state there was a reasonable firefight and that while several tanks were damaged or destroyed, the rest of the column retreated. Fred did recall that they captured several prisoners when they scoured the area. Fred always downplayed events, making them seem minor and quite humorous, clearly it was his way of recalling what were difficult memories and keeping events to himself. It's also worth bearing in mind that he had not been able to speak openly about these events for 40 years. Whether this was a coping mechanism or that his very character didn't allow him to express the real nature of events is difficult to ascertain, this writer suspects it was a bit of both.

By this point our Jed team had acquired more fighters. Added to their two companies of Corps Francs were an armed section of the Gendarmerie Maritime, 400 men who were well disciplined and very useful. A Lieutenant Peyrassol, who was known as Captain Ludovic, commanded them, the team was also joined by another group of Maquis affiliated to the FFI under the command of an Englishman. A group of Indo-Chinese had also joined them at Pertuis, with Lt Vicenzini commanding them, and they took part in 2 operations.

This unusual group took part on the 22 August in the retaking of Apt, setting up road blocks to both the south and west. This was an occasion of an issue with the FTP as they refused to cooperate as their chief had not given permission. He was 50 kilometres away and simply could not be contacted. As it turned out, the Germans had pretty much fled so it was a straightforward operation. Despite the supposed liaison between the Jeds and regular forces, it was not efficient. This was exemplified by the taking of Apt. The team received a message at 0005 on the day of the attack, stating a column was advancing from the east and north. Yet, no mention of time or any sort of co-ordination, fortunately but with great difficultly the team were able to make contact with Major Crosby who was leading the eastern column and a time was agreed for the attack.

The next day, they headed towards Lumieres and Les Baumettes where the Germans had fled to from Apt, but again by the time an attack was organised for the morning of the 24th, the Germans had moved on. By this point the team had made contact with 4SFU, the Special Forces unit which operated as a liaison between Special Forces and regular forces.

Travelling on buses packed with explosives seems to have been a normal event as on the 24th Smallwood led a patrol chasing a German detachment. Having spent the night at Cavaillon, they were among the first to enter Avignon. It had already been abandoned by the Germans so the patrol pushed on towards Orange. Unfortunately, having been misinformed as to the enemy's location the patrol was set upon at Courthezon, another episode of diving from the bus and for cover. On this occasion the bus was hit, blowing up with around 300 kilos of plastic explosive on board. This was a difficult firefight as they were surrounded by a strong German group. They eventually managed to break contact and move away with six wounded and four prisoners. An hour later the defence of Courthezon was handed over to an advancing American column.

Captain Smallwood continued reconnaissance with Paulo on the 25th, which included a visit to Colonel Saint Sauveur and continued to an attack 15 kilometres east of Montelimar. Fred commented that when Smallwood returned to Pertuis, having described how he was over extended, he was, understandably, very pleased with himself for surviving the firefight at Courthezon.

It was around this time when the regular patrols organised by Alcee picked up three German officers. It was a story which Fred recalled with some humour explaining how they had captured some Germans while out on patrol and returned them to the jail in Pertuis. Fred said some Americans turned up, drunk and wanting to shoot the Germans, while the French townsfolk wanted to hang the Germans. Fred, in typical understatement, said it was a bit of a job keeping everyone under control and not letting them get to the Germans. Clearly diplomacy was an important facet for all the team, not just Alcee. While Fred would recall these moments with great humour, it's worth considering that this team had to hold understandably furious locals at bay while also dealing with a group of gung-ho Americans who simply wanted to shoot someone. According to official reports Smallwood may not have returned by this time. This means it was likely that it was Fred and Alcee in charge of holding everyone back. Beyond this, Fred never went into details as to how they came to capture these Germans, other than they were picked up during a patrol. This would likely have involved some degree of jeopardy and the team's ability to then maintain control and order shows both courage and ingenuity. Fred discusses this incident on film which can be seen on the Legasee website, he laughs, clearly recalling the event and finding it humorous.

Captain Smallwood in his Imperial War Museum interview discusses another incident, during one of his excursions away from Pertuis. Three Germans had been captured by the Resistance who took them aside and wanted to shoot them, Smallwood attempted to dissuade them but ultimately had been unable to stop them. He referred to himself as a war criminal as clearly he felt his inability to stop the execution of these German soldiers rested with him. It was an incredibly fragile time and those on the ground aiding the French did what they could to keep situations from getting out of hand. But the French had endured so much that it was almost inevitable that there would be occasions when they metered out retribution.

Fred's role as the radio operator meant that he was to report and receive messages twice a day, but he said there were days he missed. This would be due to being out on patrol, moving around and simply on occasion lying low to avoid detection. Information though found its way to him and on one day he heard of a German column moving north from Grenoble to Lyons. He was able to get a very fast message off to Algiers requesting an air strike. In due course several Mosquito fighter bombers came in, destroying the whole convoy. Fred always remembered travelling through the area a few days later; it was hot and the bodies strewn across the road were decomposing. Fred said he never forgot that smell of death.

One sadness for Fred was the loss of one of his friends, a fellow radio operator, Dennis Gardner, known as Jess, whose parachute had failed to open. Fred found out about his death a few days after the airstrike. The news very deliberately kept from him when he was still in Algiers. Gardner was part of Team Veganin, detailed later in this chapter, they parachuted in on 8 June and while at least one of the team had returned to Algiers, they had reported that Gardner had simply stayed in France. The Resistance had buried him in one of the containers used for supply drops, in woods near Lyon. Gardner had been a good friend of Fred's and he felt compelled to locate his grave, so that it could be officially located but also so that Fred could pay his respects and be able to tell Gardner's mother. Fred and his team borrowed a jeep from a nearby American unit, who were apparently supportive of their request when told the reason. They were able to locate the grave with assistance of the Maquis who had buried him. Fred noted the grid reference, and they travelled via Lyon back to Pertuis. Fred then reported the location of the grave and always said he felt relieved at having done that. He knew that Gardner would not be forgotten. After liberation he was exhumed from his temporary resting place and reburied with Free French honours at Beaurepaire. These tragedies affected Fred and the other Jeds deeply; they had all accepted the danger but the futility of some deaths were felt more. Gardner's team, Veganin, had gone in a few months before Fred in June 1944 to the eastern side of the Rhône near Beaurepaire. With the loss of their radio operator they also lost all communication as sets were destroyed. They were reinforced a few days later by another team, Dodge, consisting of an American officer and a French-Canadian radio operator.[61]

Throughout this period, Captain Alcee had ensured patrols were sent in every direction and a few German prisoners were picked up now and then. The German retreat was not always clear and pockets of enemy soldiers remained and posed a hazard for all. Additionally Alcee spent considerable time dealing with the fragile situations between the FTP and the FFI, both Resistance groups but with opposing politics, meaning he was kept busy dealing with both politics and administration. The idea that the Jeds were to stay out of politics was not very practical, they were in the middle of various factions and simply, or perhaps not so simply, had to negotiate a way through. Also as a captain Alcee found he was outranked by many Maquis, who had acquired promotions in the field. Smallwood felt he should have held the rank Commandant, which may have aided his work and reduced many of the difficulties he encountered. This was shown by Commandant Duchene appearing in Pertuis and insisting on taking over from Captain Alcee. Duchene made what Smallwood described as a 'complete mess' of the operation on Apt. Smallwood said that Alcee spent most of his time working as a diplomat, smoothing egos and ensuring the various Resistance groups remained focused on the enemy rather than each other. This was an issue throughout France, with varying resistance groups being at odds with other groups.

This is where the tag of soldier diplomats is rooted. It must always be remembered that the Resistance was not a unified organisation, it was made of multiple groups with differing politics and ideology. Where some groups were well trained and disciplined, others were not. These groups consisted quite literally, in many cases, of the butcher, baker and maybe even a candlestick maker. They were ordinary people caught in extraordinary circumstances but determined to restore their towns and country. It was just the vision of a future France that they did not always agree on.

The team slept wherever they could, in farmhouses, often in empty shops, sometimes in the open, moving regularly. Fred said they were fortunate that they tended to get a decent warning if the Germans were headed their way, it allowed them time to move on and avoid the patrols. When Fred discussed this, he was nonchalant, as if it was perfectly normal to just move around and avoid the enemy forces. Also if the team were out on a recce or patrol they would simply phone the

---

61 Team Veganin, HS6-563

next village or town to ascertain where the enemy was. This seems almost comical but for the most part worked well. France is a large country and the Germans simply could not occupy it completely and by this point they were withdrawing. There were swathes of countryside in the South that managed to avoid too much attention. Yet, in spite of this laissez-faire attitude of the team, they did encounter the enemy multiple times. The withdrawing troops were often even more brutal and murderous during this time.

Often the Pertuis area where they were based is mentioned purely in passing, referencing the American troops and a brief mention might be made of resistance forces and those embedded with them but little more, but in spite of the briefness of their deployment, Team Citroen and so many other teams were able to assist and provide useful support and a boost to those advancing troops.

Fred states that he and the team located to Grenoble for a while and were based in a hotel there. There is no direct mention of this in the team report, but they did move around and it's more than likely that not everything was put in the report. Pertuis though seems to have been their main base.

On the 1st September contact with SFU 4 instructed them to shut down and regroup at Avignon. Fred always remembered the Hotel Crillon they all met up in, there is a poor-quality photo of Fred outside, but he always remembered they drank it dry of champagne and one suspects every other drink available.

While in Avignon Fred and others had opportunities to travel around. These however, were not jolly-boy outings.

Fred said he travelled briefly to Oradour-sur-Glane, a small village near Limoges. It had been an elegant little commune with a variety of stores that many in Limoges would travel to on the tram to do some shopping. On 10 June 1944, simply because they could, the Nazis entered the village. They rounded up all the inhabitants, men, women and children, even the infirm were roused from their beds and babies in their mother's arms. The women and children were taken to the church, the men were grouped in buildings around the village. All complied as they knew the Germans would not find anything, so thought it was simply an inconvenience. A signal was given and the soldiers opened fire on these innocent civilians, then walked among the fallen, shooting those who showed signs of life. After this the village and its inhabitants were set alight. Only a small handful survived this atrocity. When Fred walked through the village it was just a couple of months after this massacre, it was a vision which stayed with him to the end. He said he saw a sewing machine in a front window and often thought of the woman who had sat there, sewing, waving to neighbours. The horror of Oradour can still be viewed. De Gaulle declared the village must remain untouched, the blackened buildings a lesson to humanity he hoped. For those that visit even now, 80 years on, it leaves an indelible impression, just as it did for Fred all those years ago.

While the team had only been in the field for a matter of weeks, they made a difference, covering a large area. They were understandably despondent at being stood down and actually quite furious at the lateness of their deployment, a common thread for the Jeds. But Team Citroen could be proud of what they did achieve.

Fred was mentioned in despatches, his name appearing in the *London Gazette*, along with many Jedburghs, on 28 August 1945 – a year after they were in France. He always said that was for calling in the air raid on the German convoy, which ensured German reinforcements could not travel north.

There are two citations in the teams file, one for Smallwood which reads:

'Captain Smallwood was a volunteer for parachuting into France to work with the maquis. By his initiative, courage, total disregard for danger and by his high military qualities, he gained the esteem and affection of the Resistance groups under his command.

He was particularly remarkable on August 25 at Courthezon, where he succeeded, despite the inferior numbers of his group, in forcing a strong German reconnaissance unit to withdraw, and brought in his wounded and several prisoners.'

Fred's citation, dated 23 September 1944, reads:

'Volunteer for the hazardous and dangerous mission of being parachuted behind the enemy lines to the FFI as a wireless operator. For maintaining contact at all times in particularly difficult circumstances, a technician of the highest order.'

While Fred was mentioned in despatches by his own country he received the Croix de Guerre with bronze star from the French and in his later years the Légion d'honneur.

In spite of the hazardous work and perhaps because of it, comfort and friendship was taken where it could be found. Fred said he enjoyed the company of a young lady during this period in France. He never mentioned her name, although one suspects he never forgot her or her name as he would look wistful with a wry smile when mentioning her.

He promised her that he would write but of course the rest of the war got in the way and then he was home. He often expressed regret at this ungentlemanly behaviour; he presumed and hoped she found happiness after the war. Fred was very discreet and never divulged any details but love affairs during turbulent times are often enjoyed in the moment and the reality of normal life means they are best left as joyful memories.

Fred would only occasionally dwell on the more difficult moments of the war. He would comment that he witnessed some terrible, quite sickening sights, from the aftermath of the airstrike he called in to the retribution directed at those who had been believed to collaborate with the Nazis. He didn't go into details of what he saw, but history is full of stories and photos exist of punishment being meted out. Punishment, particularly towards women, seems rooted in the dark ages, heads shaved as a public humiliation. Often these women were targeted as having been *collaborators horizontale* and no doubt a number of women did have relationships with German soldiers, but even cleaners at German headquarters were targeted as well as women who had German soldiers forcibly billeted in their homes. It is argued by some that this violence was a sign of jealousy, many of these women having been able to access food and enjoyed entertainment because of their associations with the enemy. Many died during these reprisals and a good proportion were women.

There is one photo of Fred which causes great discussion, well the badge on his beret causes the discussion. Fred was very good at evading questions or claiming not to remember how he acquired the badge. One day though in his final couple of years, I asked him for the umpteenth time about the photo and the badge. He quite nonchalantly said 'Oh I took that off an SS officer I shot'. I was so surprised at his apparent candour that I simply said 'OK I broached the subject the following day but Fred simply said, 'Oh no, that's not right, I forget now' and attempted to recant his earlier candour. There continues to be a query over this badge and clearly we will never know the truth, but I do wonder if that moment of candour and letting his guard down was accurate. There were moments when we spoke when you could almost see him thinking as to whether to say something but his discipline always kicked in and he kept his own counsel on, it is presumed, many incidents and encounters.

Three other teams dropped into France on the same night as Fred and Team Citroen. All four were based in Algiers and flew out from Blida on the same evening. These teams were Cinnamon, Monocle and Spectre and they all had interesting deployments.

Team Monocle

This three-man team, of Captain J Tossel, Lieutenant R H Foster and Sergeant R J Andersen found themselves in an important location and were able to support and assist the Maquis in constant guerrilla action disrupting enemy communications.[62] Dropping the same night as Fred and Team Citroen, flying like Team Citroen in a Liberator, they were located to the Drome region. They dropped on the same ground as Fred, their first site too dangerous, the drop was not good. It was from too high and rather than flying in on the lights they flew across them. Tosel landed safely on the edge of the field with Anderson landing on the opposite edge of a field but Foster found himself 300 yards down in a valley and suffered a sprained ankle and damaged knee. Their containers, dropped from too high as seems to have happened too often meant they were scattered over a wide area. These errors were not just irritating but also dangerous for the teams and the maquis on the ground, having to spend time locating and retrieving vital supplies. As in Team Citroen, the drop zone was for equipment not men and the reception committee were not expecting them. Archiduc met them as he did Team Citroen and the team moved to Archiduc's camp, where they met up with Team Citroen and one suspects traded landing experiences. At the camp they also met Colonel Constans and Major Crosby. The following day they were provided with men to help them locate their containers. They commented on 10 American airmen in the camp who provided useful assistance and mentioned seeing Captain Laubier, who had an OG (Operational Group) group.

Their initial instructions were to contact Major Legrande, who was the chief of the Free French in the Drome region. They set off two days later, in a truck provided by the Free French and were given a good supply of arms and ammunition. At Buy de Baronies they were able to provide American weapons and give instructions on American demolitions to the 1st Bn of the FTP.

Anderson stated that his radio container was found in perfect condition, which given Citroen's experience was very lucky. On the second day he mentions that Fred used his set to try to establish contact but that he was not able to do so. Anderson made contact three days later, and found he could hear Algiers best during the morning. He was very dissatisfied with the operator on the base emergency frequency, as it seems he had to repeat messages several times. Nonetheless, he conveyed in his report that he found his radio set very satisfactory

---

62 Team Monocle, HS6-545

but the procedure from base left a lot to be desired; it was particularly irritating to be asked to repeat a message when they should have known that once transmitted the message was destroyed. Anderson also made the comment that startling Q signals were used.

They made contact with Major Legrand on 16 August. Tosel and Foster hurried to see him, but while they worked with him it seems he was quite difficult to get on with. Captain Tosel seems to have had to spend time explaining things to the Major.

They were able to distribute their equipment which was put to good use. They found an isolated spot around 12 kilometres from the headquarters, and situated their radio there, it appears that one officer stayed at this location. Tosel appears to have stayed at the Free French headquarters, which were located at the Chateau de la Vachere, north of Blancon. Daytime would see them keeping an eye on important routes including the route along the Rhône. Nighttime would see one of the officers accompanying the Free French, offering assistance and supporting ambush and sabotage efforts. Foster kept an eye on the aerodrome near Chabieul for three days and this successfully resulted in an attack on the gasoline dump.

They listened out for instructions on the BBC and heard an instruction to intensify work on the communications in the area. They did this, destroying phone lines, using those who worked there. Power lines were destroyed again by workers in Bezancon. The rail line between Livron and Veynes was cut with 17 kilometres of rail removed and the rails moved into the mountains to prevent them being reinstalled. While the rail line between Valence and Avignon was cut multiple times, the Germans repaired it each time immediately. Every night attacks were carried out on the main Route National 7 along the Rhône with the bridge at Livron being cut. The river was passable but traffic was disrupted with only 4 trucks an hour able to cross. The result being that the Germans would only travel on Route 7 during the day and suspended night traffic after 20 August. The team were also involved in attacking the German headquarters at Chateau de Montellier with good results.

They had in the Free French good numbers spread across the region and were able to ensure that they were used efficiently both before and after the Americans arrived. There were a few thousand in specific FFI and FTP groups along with around 500 men in Valence and 300 in Montelimar.

The Americans arrived on 22 August and the team's work shifted from active to more liaison and information gathering for the Americans. Captain Tosel worked with one unit of Americans who arrived at the

Free French headquarters while Lieutenant Foster returned with the Lieutenant of their reconnaissance battalion to their headquarters to provide information on the area.

The Free French from this point started to pick up anyone suspicious which helped the advance. The team had phone communication with Vallence and the agents in place provided precise information on enemy positions. The team also managed to get detailed information on the La Tresorie aerodrome at Valence, which they passed on to the 509 Engineer Battalion. As well as this, several women would cross the German lines daily and report back which provided more valuable information for the advancing troops. At this point the Free French concentrated their efforts around Valence, the Americans bypassed this town, with the Germans withdrawing, the Free French went in and cleared remaining enemy elements and took around 1000 prisoners. A roadblock south of Livron placed by the Butler force ensured with the arrival of the 26th Division and assistance from the Free French that many German trucks and equipment were destroyed. The Americans liberated Romans with the Free French following to take over.

Foster, having found Legrande cold, seems to have attempted to work on freeing Major Manner who had been captured near Romans on 6 August. He details his investigation, realising that the Major could have been rescued from Valence where the Milice were holding him but this wasn't done in time. He was then taken by the Gestapo ultimately to Belfort. Foster had a plan to buy him out of prison as this would apparently have worked but he was ordered back to Grenoble by Major Bonner of the OSS.

The team was very effective, in spite of a poor drop, specifying no reception committee and receiving nothing in terms of supply drops. It seems that they felt that Commandant Legrande was not keen on Americans and that this may have been the reason for his cold attitude.

As seen too often with the Jed teams, poor drops caused unnecessary problems and it seems that as well trained as the radio operators in the field were, it was not always the case for those at base.

Team Sceptre

Team Sceptre was despatched to the Alpes Maritimes to work along the French-Italian border. Lieutenant W C Hanna, Lieutenant F Trevenac and Sergeant Palmer, who replaced the original team member, Sgt. Tracey, before despatch, suffered a poor landing like too many teams.[63] This resulted in Trevenac suffering a broken foot and

---

63 Team Sceptre, HS6-557

the radio operator, Palmer, spraining his knee. The radio was slightly damaged in the drop and it was noted that the field was miserable and not suited to dropping personnel. Their first priorities became finding a doctor to set the broken foot and organising transport to move their stores to a suitable location. Due to a lack of transport they decided to locate within the general area and set up camp around 5 miles north of Fayence. They distributed equipment and arranged ambush patrols in the area. They collected 10 British parachutists along with an injured British officer, this stated without any further explanation. In spite of obvious issues around injury and transport they seem to have made the best of the situation and were able to coordinate with the Resistance and organise patrols. At some point a British captain arrived and took the 10 parachutists but then 3 American parachutists arrived. Ongoing patrols ensured that, as the team put it, activity began. As the Germans withdrew, they were able with the Maquis to capture 190 prisoners, 300 were killed and there were 28 casualties. They also listed 6 vehicles as being destroyed. They comment on losing contact with 517th Parachute Regiment around Gallain, so it would seem that they were working in support of the advancing troops as per their original plan. They did plan an attack on Fayence, but the Maquis had to fall back to protect other towns as the Germans retreated but continued to attack. The team organised the blowing up of two bridges, using two of the Americans to assist the maquis, they prepared a third bridge. This action resulted in the capture of 45 prisoners, 18 were killed and there were 3 casualties in the maquis.

They contacted a German officer to discuss terms as they planned another attack on Fayence, which resulted in the Germans surrendering with no casualties on either side; 187 prisoners were taken with over 200 weapons and 4 vehicles. The three Americans were commended by the team for their assistance. Hanna was recommended for a decoration by Major Marten stating that dictating the terms of the German surrender saved at least 100 Americans lives. Palmer was also recommended for a decoration following this engagement. They had sent a messenger to the 517th and they then moved into Fayence, having given information on the area they prepared to move north. However, they were ordered to 4 SFU (Special Forces Unit) for an urgent mission. They moved equipment and men to Brignoles. At this stage they met Captain Harcourt and formed a new partnership with his French officer, Captain Perandon. They travelled to Grasse to the headquarters of the 11th Airborne Division with the aim of incorporating American paratroopers into the team and they were successful in releasing a number of paratroops to their team. For three days they collected supplies and awaited orders. After 3 days of waiting the team was disbanded with the paratroopers sent back to their regiment, Hanna was given an assignment as a liaison officer, with Lieutenant Teverac sent to Corsica he had been injured and was like Hanna recommended for decoration. All supplies were given away. It is very clear that Hanna was unhappy, he says he became disgusted and left Brignoles with Palmer and accompanied Lieutenant Mackintosh to Gap on a mission. After this they moved north to Briancon and joined Lieutenant Generich, once that work was complete they returned to headquarters now located in Grenoble to await any further developments.

All teams gave suggestions in their reports and Hanna's like many pulls no punches. He states that there needed to be some plan for the immediate future of teams once they were overrun rather than, in his words ' let them die of neglect and old age within a strange land, forgotten and discarded by their own headquarters'. He comments around rank, this team had 2 lieutenants and it would seem that this may have caused some issues as Hanna says 'The rank of each officer in the team should be a captaincy at the minimum to avoid petty misunderstandings which frequently occur when a superior officer fails to condescend to a junior officer's suggestions'. He also says to dispose of the all-hush-hush Jed hypocrisy, and give information to relevant individuals in the attacking forces. This was an issue; the Jeds were so secret the following troops had no idea who or what they were. There were other complaints around unnecessary repetition of messages and care needed at base to select the correct one-time pads.

Additionally, the radio operators' report comments on the damage to the set on landing, and there was criticism of base operators, Palmer giving the example of being within sight of Germans yet it took the base operator 30 minutes to retune his transmitter. He also commented on the noise the generator made which made it unsafe close to the enemy.

The three Americans, Hackard, De Shayes and Hughes who had found themselves with the team and stayed, were also recommended for decorations as they volunteered to stay with the team and assist in the continuing harrassment of the enemy.

They had suffered an inauspicious start with their poor landing, yet achieved a great deal and endured a difficult deployment.

Official records show Hanna and Palmer returning from France within a day of each other in September 1944. It is assumed the French member of the team remained in France.

Team Cinnamon

This team consisted of two French men and one British (often the misconception with the Jedburghs is that all teams consisted of one French, one British and one American),[64] Lieutenant F L Ferandon, Captain R Harcourt, Corporal J Maurin, suffered a seriously bad landing with Captain Harcourt landing hard in trees and breaking both legs. This again was due to a poor drop, too fast with a premature green light to jump. While the drop zone was long, planted with lavender and clear, the fast inaccurate drop meant that they landed 400 metres to the right of the actual drop zone, so Captain Harcourt landed in trees rather than clear ground, although fortunately the other two members of the team landed in clearings. Nonetheless another poor drop with Captain Harcourt, quite understandably, furious, stating in his report that he could not be more angry. Both he and Corporal Maurin stated that they somersaulted in the air, which they had never done before and Captain Ferandon said he was pushed. Like Fred and Team Citroen, they dropped to the Perpendiculaire circuit in the Var region. Beyond the injury, their containers had landed fairly accurately, yet they had the Verey ammunition and Team Citroen had the pistols.

A British Major, known as Firmin, was with the reception committee, they managed to move Captain Harcourt to a copse and he was able to discuss the possibilities within the area, which shows great courage as he must have been in agony. There had been many clashes in the south since 6 June and this did complicate matters. The Major explained that one Maquis group had been dispersed by the enemy. A proposal to locate a headquarters and begin to build a group was felt by Harcourt to be too long term and not practical in the fast moving situation around them, they didn't have enough potential personnel and with a scarcity of food as well as the high price of food, it simply was not practical. Firmin was concerned with Marseille and wanted to get back there.

The team's contact was Colonel Gouzy who they understood to have a safe house in St Maximin, however, they were advised that the Germans had taken the town and were using the previous safe house, Gouzy had retired to Varages. They sent a member of the reception team to fetch the Colonel and he duly appeared the next morning and was able to provide the team with accurate information. Of the two rail lines they had studied it transpired that one was not used and the other only used for transporting basalt, so they abandoned

---

64 Team Cinnamon, HS6-496

the idea of attacking them. Gouzy had 12 groups of guerrillas each led by an officer so the team felt these were the people to work with and thought concentrating efforts on roads and bridges would be the best use of everyone's efforts. Lieutenant Pavlovitch appeared after Gouzy and while he possessed a lot of information he lacked the military understanding of the problems being faced. The team now had choices to make, while Captain Harcourt favoured an option of trying to get both Gouzy and Pavlovitch's teams to work together, Captain Ferandon preferred to have his headquarters at Pavolvitch's house in Seillons.

Captain Harcourt was out of action, so he yielded to Ferandon's preferences. The Captain was transported with Madame Gouzy to a farm, a surgeon was brought in and his leg was set, albeit temporarily. He had to be moved after a few days, as suspicion was aroused, and he was taken to another house on the other side of Varages and continued to be cared for by Maquis members while the other two members of the team worked with the Maquis groups in the area mopping up enemy combatants in pockets around the area. In spite of being out of action, Captain Harcout found himself in the thick of it when the Germans moving through started firing at the house. A battle ensued with Captain Harcourt being carried out of the house into woods at the back. As time passed American troops arrived to support the guerrillas. Once peace descended the Captain was taken briefly to the 10th American Field Hospital for further treatment but returned to, as he said, French friends until he transferred to Special Forces Unit 4 at Brignoles. Due to his continuing immobility he worked in the office until he could move around and then managed to travel across South East and South West France contacting Jedburgh teams and others. It was not the outcome the Captain had worked for, the poor drop costing him the opportunity to work in the field and denying those in the field of a valuable well-trained commando.

The French officer, Captain Ferandon, gave a very detailed account of the operation. The French radio operator's report was short and to the point. He was highly critical that inexperienced operators were used at base. He commented on incomprehensible messages and exaggerated repetitions were enough to tire out an operator in the field. Like Fred, he had used his Jed set as his B2 set had also been damaged during the initial drop. He made a point of mentioning his admiration for Captain Harcourt, following his severe injury, and Captain Ferrandon who he stated was a magnificent trainer. He clearly had the utmost respect for both men. Once the team was stood down, he went to Marseille and Toulouse to carry on working this time for Major Ougnon and Captain Eydoux.

Additionally they worked to demolish bridges and were able to pass on useful information to troops as they came into the area.

The fury of the team and particularly Captain Harcourt reflects a serious issue that the Jedburghs faced. The secrecy of their unit and training and objectives meant no-one knew who they were or appreciated the need for good safe drops. The pilots who caused the injuries and even death for those who had spent months in specialised training are hard to forgive. While in the midst of war, situations can be tense and difficult, these pilots were we assume ill informed about the process of dropping these chaps as the alternative that a more cavalier attitude was present as the end of the war loomed is quite troublesome.

The aforementioned demonstrates the very real risk that the Jeds undertook, they are sometimes regarded as soldiers who simply played at war, but they were not. They always downplayed the risks and brushed off the dangers, but they were in dangerous situations and some paid with their lives. Their humble nature and often reluctance to speak of their experiences has allowed some to undervalue their contributions.

The Jedburghs, once deployed, suffered in terms of supplies; so many demands and limited aircraft meant that often it was the Jed teams that lost out. It's interesting that when they could speak of their experiences they did not hold back on criticisms. Of course, the issue was that no-one could anticipate the level of speed of the invasion either in the north or eventually in the south. The speed of the invasion meant that many Jeds were simply overrun which goes to the argument that they should have been sent in sooner. Nonetheless, multiple teams achieved great results.

Other teams dropped from Algiers are discussed in the appendix.

The post-war situation in France would prove to be quite complex, there was a jealousy and suspicion around the SOE F Section that lingered. F Section had proved itself very efficient and proficient, more equipment was landed to this section than to the BCRA circuits and this fuelled jealousy. France wanted and needed to say it had freed itself and it could not, so it turned on its friend. Additionally the communist groups who had proved difficult during the war now viewed the old F Section as right wing and a danger to them. While the communists had often caused issues it is worth remembering that the British did arm them while the French BCRA would not; they always kept a wary eye, aware of possible post-war repercussions.

For the Jedburghs, some completed more than one mission to France and some stayed on to train officers for the French Army. For most though, including Fred, they left and only returned as civilians in later years. The wider SOE were aware of potential dangers to those who had worked as agents, and employed the Judex mission to smooth potential issues. British officers from SOE headquarters made two tours of France, meeting with the various circuits and members to thank and congratulate them as well as ensuring they gained the appropriate accreditation for their roles in securing freedom for France. F Section had sent in 393 agents of which 119 were arrested or killed. Only 17 who were arrested came back. It was a high cost but one which each agent took on knowingly and willingly.

De Gaulle's attitude towards the Allies as his country was liberated did not help; soldiers who had liberated his country were unwelcome and dismissed as a nuisance. He wanted and needed to be the conquering hero and did not want to acknowledge the allies and their vital role in freeing his country, it is with hindsight an understandable requirement for the morale and rebuilding of France, to feel she had gained her own independence. Nonetheless it soured relations particularly between Britain and France.

A BRIEF HOP TO ITALY

It's fair to say that all the Jedburghs who met up in Avignon had stories to tell and they enjoyed their brief R&R at the Hotel Crillon. While there a call went out from Neil Marten for three radio operators to head to Italy for an operation urgently.

Fred along with Ted Cornick and Thomas 'Cobber' Cain stuck their hands up and were duly despatched. Fred recounted a fairly miserable overnight journey down to Marseille, acorn coffee but nothing to eat. Acorn coffee was very much part of wartime life, not the best coffee, in fact not coffee at all being made from acorns, but it was abundant during the war. They arrived at an airfield which had been all but destroyed and waited. Eventually a Dakota arrived and transported them to Bari on the eastern coast of Italy, where Fred said no-one was expecting them; he seemed to find this news inevitable. After some time they were transported to, in Fred's words, a god-forsaken town called Monopoli with Number 1 Special Force. Monopoli had been the SOE base, very roughly between Bari to the north and Brindisi to the south. but does seem to have gained something of a reputation, a song 'Monopoli Blues' was penned and suggests it might not have been the happiest of locations. Despite the apparent urgency suggested at Avignon, there was no clear plan, the men were told there were operations in Italy and Austria, Fred making specific mention of an operation to Austria. But without clear information and by this time the men were appropriately fed up, they refused to engage with any operation. The camp adjutant apparently told them they could take the operation or stay where they were and bloody well rot. The issue with operations into Austria and indeed Germany was speed, things were moving at pace and as good as the SOE had become, setting up and dropping into either Austria or Germany was impractical. The idea of agents and on-the-ground resistance simply was not cultivated in these countries that offered any positive benefits. Fred never mentioned the name of the person but variously said he was the camp adjutant or colonel in different interviews, likely he was a colonel who was the adjunct as well. This was during the time that Gerry Holdsworth was in charge of Special Force No 1. He would go on to found the Holdsworth Trust, which continues today with the aim of preserving and promoting the heritage of SOE and the wider Special Forces.

Just after this encounter one of the famed Jed stories occurred. Tommy MacPherson and Oscar Brown arrived before heading off to North Italy. Oscar took the opportunity to engage the chaps in some poker and duly stripped them of all their cash; one imagines it was quite the encounter as it passed into history. This is perhaps why Fred never, when we knew him, engaged in any form of gambling during the rest of his life, never a lottery ticket bought or a bet on a horse placed. Some weeks passed before Roger Leney and Geoff Hallowes came through on their way back to the UK. Fred and his comrades begged them to inform Baker Street of their location and get them out. Fortunately Roger and Geoff were able to relay the message and Baker Street sent a request for their presence in London. There followed a boat crossing from Bari to Alexandria, a train ride to Cairo and then a three-week break, described by Fred as a pleasant sightseeing visit. Fred also said that they were not keen on the barracks in Abbasiya so located themselves in a small hotel in what Fred described as the seamy end of Cairo. Cairo was fading at this time; it had been a focal point in the early days of the war, but at the point Fred was there, it would have been reeling from the assassination of Lord Moyne. He had been murdered by the Stern Group, fighters for a free Isreal. Moyne was blamed for a decision in 1940, when Churchill and Eden had agreed to the formation of a Jewish army, with up to 10,000 men. Unfortunately, Churchill had not sought approval for this plan before giving his word. Political and economic decisions meant that the Palestine administration and the Commander in the Middle East could not be persuaded to agree to a Jewish army, and it fell to Lord Moyne to deliver the bad news. At the time most, including the Jewish community, viewed the Stern Group as terrorists but decades later those who murdered Lord Moyne were buried with full military honours among the founders of Israel. Fred made no mention of tensions in Cairo, it might just have been another factor in a time of war. Fred and his friends though seemed to have a jolly time in Cairo in spite of any problems and it must have been a welcome time of rest and a bit of fun. Following this break, they caught a ship at Alexandria on Christmas Eve 1944 and had a two-week journey back to England.

It is an interesting facet of the Jedburghs that they had some autonomy; this had been clear from the days at Milton Hall with the dropping of salutes and parades. These men were being asked to think for themselves on the ground without any immediate command, so it was inevitable that if they didn't like something they wouldn't do it. So whatever might have awaited them in Austria, they chose not to get involved. Fred, as staid and sensible as he was, had little time for fools and he certainly seemed to feel that the hierarchy had its fair share.

Once back in London, Fred was given the stark choice, volunteer for Force 136 in the Far East or return to your regiment. This choice had been delivered to many in Avignon but Fred and his friends having hopped to Italy had delayed this ultimatum. There was no choice for Fred or indeed many Jeds, no way was Fred heading back to the Green Howards, so a long voyage beckoned. This was the choice faced by all the Jeds and a very good number of the British Jeds went on to join Force 136. The American Jeds were returned either to their units or back to the States, but many found their way to the Far East, and for the French Jeds, many continued to fight for France in the Indo-China region.

CHAPTER FOUR

BURMA AND MALAYA

The Japanese carried out targeted and planned attacks and invasions from Pearl Harbor to Hong Kong, Singapore, Burma and Malaya during December 1941. This development would see the war rage in these territories for years and extend beyond the end of the war in Europe.

Fred's decision to join Force 136 was a very clear choice to engage in more action. The Jeds were so well trained and ready for action and many felt they had been under-utilised in Europe so it's hardly surprising that so many volunteered for duty in the Far East.

While the political landscape of Burma is beyond the scope of this work, the story in the Far East was very different to France or indeed Europe. In France they were clearly going to liberate a country invaded by an aggressor. However, in the Far East the Japanese had declared themselves the liberators, freeing people from imperial control. The empires of particularly Britain and France were a more complex theatre. This issue caused significant issues with the Americans, who wanted to free these countries but were very clear that they did not want them returned to European empires. Official records are littered with correspondence which shows the uneasy relationship between the allies in this theatre of war.[65] The clear anti-colonial views of the Americans caused issues throughout the region. While the Japanese had declared themselves the liberators and were initially met either with apathy or even welcomed, they soon showed themselves to be a brutal force. While this made the Allies welcome in most arenas, there was unease. The assistance of the Allies was welcome but it was not just the Americans who did not want to return to colonial power.

---

65 Richard Duckett, *The Special Operations Executive in Burma*, London: Bloomsbury, 2022, pp.27-45

The SOE, in preparation for a potential war with Japan, had set up the Oriental Mission in May 1941. The problem was that it was based on the European model of country stations, but for the Far East this was a flawed idea. To begin with the mission covered an enormous range of territories. It was also assumed that there would be a level of co-operation from both civil and military authorities. The issue with this was a lack of resources and co-operation. Valentine Killery, who had been despatched as head of the mission, put together a plan for small teams to be inserted and if necessary left behind with weapons to aid a resistance. While he hoped to organise the mission within a year, it became clear that he lacked co-operation from those who could aid the mission. The SOE idea of ungentlemanly warfare was so alien to those on the ground that co-operation did not come easily if at all.

Beyond this was a multitude of difficulties, the climate, a predominantly jungle environment with monsoons meant that any theatre of war was so different to Europe that tactics could not be transplanted. Add to this a population who, in many cases, were either apathetic or even hostile and the British found themselves in a precarious position.

Finally, communications were difficult, London was a world away with little to no understanding of the circumstances on the ground. As if all this was not enough, add in that SOE was not officially recognised and was still trying to find its feet in Europe let alone in distant lands.

Unfortunately bickering between those who perhaps should have known better meant that Killery's plan simply did not happen and by the time the Japanese invaded and the realisation of the value of such a plan, it was too late.

Nevertheless, this was not the end and a number of men ranging from planters to civil servants were given a crash course at an isolated peninsula near Singapore, known as STS 101.[66] A small number of teams were able to locate to areas the Japanese had not yet reached, areas already under Japanese control could not be reached.

The British left Burma in 1942, after a series of what could politely be called misunderstandings which stretched from SOE through to the military and the civil authorities, as well as the issues previously mentioned. Yet in spite of the long list of problems, they left behind agents and in fact groups of agents who were entrusted with keeping lines of communication open to provide information with the hope that the British would return. The speed of the advancing Japanese coupled

---

66 Ibid, p.53

with the small groups left behind, meant that in six months Britain had lost most of Burma. Official reports following the British leaving Burma states that the impact of SOE was slight but perhaps underestimates the impact they had. The sabotage ensured the Japanese did not have a clear run to the north of the country. While this was a limited impact at the time, more delaying than anything, it also prevented the Japanese creating a fighter strip at Fort Hertz which allowed an air bridge to remain for supplies between India and China. So, while limited, the impact assisted in specific areas.[67]

Perhaps one of the best known soldiers from this period was Major Hugh Seagram. He was left behind in the area of Papun. He trained many locals but encountered the not-unknown SOE problem of a lack of arms. He eventually went into hiding with the Karen people and continued to do what he could to thwart the Japanese. He stayed with the Karen people until 1944, when the Japanese began reprisals knowing that he was in the area. He surrendered to stop reprisals against villagers and along with others was taken to Rangoon and was executed by the Japanese.[68] While he had been hindered by a lack of arms and communications, he and others throughout the region had slowed the Japanese onslaught. Force 136 would have to pick up the threads of previous efforts and work to gain the trust and assistance of the locals.

Fred boarded a troopship, HMS *Chitral*, in Liverpool, having enjoyed a couple of weeks leave and sailed for Calcutta.[69] He joked that there was a great block of concrete on the aft of the ship upon which sat a 6in gun, which he laughed about wondering what bright spark had thought that would ever be any use. Fred said the ship pitched terribly, possibly due to the chunk of concrete on the aft deck. It took four or five weeks to sail there, Fred made little comment but others have commented on passing Gibraltar. This proved a brief but welcome highlight in the journey with lights and a band playing on the shore as they arrived at this British outpost. It would have been a very welcome sight for the soldiers who lined the deck and enjoyed the view well into the evening. The journey though was uneventful and once in Calcutta, Fred had a 5-day train journey and a ferry ride to arrive at their new if temporary base. There was a period of acclimatisation as well as jungle training.

---

67 Charles Cruickshank, *Special Operations Executive in the Far East*, Oxford: Oxford University Press, 1986, p.69

68 Duckett, *The Special Operations Executive in Burma*, p. 119

69 Personal comms.

This was also where Fred met his new teammates. Fred was trained at M.E. 25 once the teams were set. From 19 March until 12 April, they went through a series of exercises, both to alclimatise and to help them get used to their new team. Fred was attached to the Nation Operation, with Team Cow which consisted of Major D C 'Paddy' McCoull and Captain Jimmy Allen-Mirehouse, who Fred always said enjoyed a good joke and was a good companion, and of course Fred as radio operator.

Once ready the team travelled by train back to Calcutta to await orders and final briefings. There is evidence that briefings were fairly useless, with several saying it would have been better if those giving the briefings had admitted they knew nothing. This was also the point that they met their two Burmese guides, Kin Saw and Ba Maung/UBau Maung. Kin Saw would be their translator as his English was particularly good.

Fred often commented on his kit for Burma, which was far superior in quality to that which he had been supplied for France. He was delighted that his rucksack was waterproof, which meant that in the jungle, he had a hope of keeping some possessions dry. He also remembered his jungle canvas boots, which he seemed to think would not last very long. The following is taken from personal recollections of Fred as well as official reports.

Fred was dropped into Burma overnight on 30 April 1945, with the objective of capturing a town called Thaton.[70] The team were dropped to meet Team Giraffe, which consisted of Major McAdam, Sub Lieutenant Moore, Sgt. Edgar and U San Tint. Fred referred to Major MacAdam as Mac and said he was a funny chap.

While this was another drop from a Liberator, unlike France this drop was without significant incident. It was flown by a British crew and Fred said they jumped in fighting order, just in case of trouble. Major McCoull landed on the drop zone with Fred and the rest of the team landing in scrub nearby, in fact Fred said he landed in sapling trees which bent and helped break his fall, the issue being that the drop zone was particularly small. Team Giraffe had dropped in just a couple of nights earlier and their landing was heavy with their guide suffering a sprained ankle which meant he was out of action for a month. Team Giraffe had been met by Team Rabbit who had dropped blind in March and scouted the area and were able to confirm that the locals were friendly. They had established the camp for the initial arrival of Giraffe and due to the short notice of Team Cow's arrival the same drop zone and initial camp were used.

---

70 National Archive file HS1

Once they gathered their kit and equipment they had a march of a few hours through the jungle to reach camp at Saw Bali Creek. Fred said, at this point, he felt relatively safe, in spite of being behind enemy lines, he and his team felt protected by the thick jungle.

The aim for Teams Cow and Giraffe was to report intelligence in the area and to arm and train the Burmese National Army members and the levies engaged by the British. They were also to control these forces, which was a significant undertaking for two small teams of 3. They were given an operating area which bounded Thaton on the west, their target and Salween on the east. While the team had undergone jungle training and acclimatisation, their briefing was less thorough, with official documents stating a very rough preliminary briefing was carried out while they were at M.E.25. What was described as a proper briefing took place in Calcutta with Major Battersby, yet inadequate information about other Force 136 teams was given. Both Team Cow and Team Giraffe were left with the impression that there were no other teams operating within 100 miles of them. Yet records show there were a number of teams within their section of the Nation area.

For Fred and Team Cow they had, in fact, originally been aiming for an area south of Rangoon, but owing to the advance of the 14th Army their target area was switched, as they awaited despatch from Jessore, and they had no briefing at all on where they were going. Their original briefing paper states they were dropping to Station Yak, which Team Panda had dropped to a few weeks previously. Naturally all the information they had was based on this briefing paper and any verbal briefing they received. Fortunately as Team Giraffe met them, they were able to give them some information. But as they noted in the official report, had they been dropped to another drop zone, without the benefit of another team meeting them, they would have, in their understated words, had difficulties. This continues with the typical Jed attitude of underplaying risks and the often scant information available to teams as they deployed.

The camp, when they arrived, consisted of several huts on stilts with a bamboo floor. It was somewhat dilapidated so the team set about fixing it up. The creek that ran through the camp provided water, although unlike the Burmese, the team used chlorine purification tablets to ensure the water was safe for them to drink. What was not immediately apparent to them was that there was a Japanese camp quite close to their location. Fred said initially there were about 35 men there to work with them. But the Burmese National Army mutinied and around 200 joined their camp.

McCoull carried out his first night recce with McAdam on the night of 4 May. The following day Moore of Team Giraffe left for Zokala with 70 weapons for the BNA in the area. He was able to send letters back and advise that while the area was very hot with enemy activity he would stay as it would be useful for intelligence purposes.

On 6 May group of BNA (Burmese National Army) working out of the teams camp ambushed at long range a group of 47 Japanese, killing 3 and wounded 5 while remaining free of casualties themselves. The following night saw them ambush more Japanese, on this occasion managing to capture 7 rifles and grenades, the BNA suffered one wounded in this attack which saw 2 Japanese killed.

On 8 May, McCoull, Allan Mirehouse and Edgar took a party of 15 BNA down to the road at Mogaung hoping to catch a group of Japanese who would be isolated, which seemed to be a popular method of movement at night time. Fred with his radio would have stayed at camp; often the radio operator or in this case at least one would be protected given their importance in communications. The party duly arrived at their chosen location but it was a heavily populated area and their location very close to the road making it almost impossible for them to stay out of sight of houses. Many of these houses they knew were being occupied by Japanese troops. Unfortunately for the group one of the BNA soldiers dropped his Sten gun and fired off one round. As they had no clear intelligence as to the location of enemy troops they withdrew. This day was VE Day and Europe was celebrating but for Fred and his comrades, the war was far from over. Fred recalled the message coming through about VE Day which was likely a day or two later, it instructed them to celebrate in their jungle camp. Fred was unimpressed often saying that those sending the message clearly had no clue as to what was going on, but nevertheless the team was able to enjoy a laugh about it, although they did not celebrate.

The following night another ambush at Kinmongyon killed 3 Japanese officers and 15 other ranks.

10 May saw Fred getting out on a recce with McCoull. They observed movements along the road at Padeynyo overnight from a distance of 10 yards. This intelligence gathering was one of their primary roles as well as arming and training the locals. Two days later on the 12th a party of 26 INA (Indian National Army) soldiers surrendered to the teams and retrieved 6 rifles.

After a couple of weeks in the jungle Fred said he was the fittest he had ever been. They had some fresh rations and their K rations. The K rations were American and according to Roger Leney consisted of morning and evening rations, containing items such as Spam, biscuits, chocolate, a few cigarettes and even some toilet paper.[71] Fred slept on the floor of his hut under a mosquito net and seems to have been quite content with his posting, certainly initially at least enjoying being in the jungle. By this point someone had invented a steam generator to run his radio set. He thought this genius since so long as he had water and fire he could always communicate with HQ. If they needed anything, whether ammunition, boots or food, a call went in and a couple of days later a drop would deliver supplies. During these early weeks, according to Fred, all was going well.

He did recall that while the team were well aware of the suffering of the locals at the hands of the Japanese, and they wanted to encourage them to fight. This was a delicate situation, newcomers attempting to encourage fighting against an enemy who had shown their brutality. Yet it seems that McCoull treaded diplomatically and was able to encourage them. Fred remembered one day, when on the radio, one of their levies rolled up calling out 'Freddy, Freddy!' Fred turned around to see this man, apparently very happy and proud who proceeded to lift up his arms and show Fred two severed heads.[72] Fred said he managed to mutter a 'well done' to the chap before telling him 'for God's sake go and bury them'. He said he was sure his jaw had dropped to the floor with shock at this event and it was an image which he tried to forget.

Fred noticed that a number of the levies within their camp were in poor health and requested medical supplies for them. In doing this, with his 4 hours of first aid training at Milton Hall, he became the camp doctor. He started when one of the levies had a boil behind his ear and Fred lanced it and the chap improved. This caused a knock-on effect and Fred found he had lines of people queuing up to see him and cure them of their various ills. While Fred found it hard work but rewarding, it helped the team embed and the locals looked upon them even more favourably. It also gave Fred something positive to focus on in later years, he knew he had provided help to many during this time. It was noted more generally that first aid and medical assistance given by the teams in Burma was a great boost, giving confidence to the locals and gaining loyalty so those 4 hours of first-aid training at Milton Hall proved very worthwhile. While Fred was able to help many of the levies and locals with health issues, often foot problems, he couldn't always help. The team noticed that the locals when faced

---

71 Roger Leney, *Mongoose White, Behind Enemy Lines in Burma*, courtesy of Simon Leney
72 Personal comms and Sean Rayment, *Tales from the Special Forces Club*, London: Collins, 2013, p.250

with something unknown were prone to taste it; unfortunately one local got hold of a stick of plastic explosive, he duly tasted it and in Fred's words 'went off his rocker'. Fred tried everything to calm the chap, ultimately giving him a small dose of morphine, but sadly he died a day later. These losses stayed with Fred, although he knew he had done all he could. He commented that while he had seen death and dead bodies in France, he still found it shocking and he was after all only 21 at this time. So young yet he had already seen more than many would see in a lifetime.

On the 16 May Moore, a Royal Naval volunteer reservist, who had stayed for intelligence purposes around Zokala, evacuated a Lieutenant Commander Leslie and 3 ratings whose MTB (Motor Torpedo Boat) had capsized while in the mouth of the Sittang River. He evacuated them by sampan (flat-bottomed boat) to Rangoon. Moore was then sent back in to join Major Lucas of Mongoose Blue, part of the Character operation.[73]

For the following week, the BNA group were unrelenting in their ambushing of the enemy on the Bilin to Thaton road. During this week on the 22nd McAdam had taken 10 levies with him to recce the Salween area. In spite of the BNA and their active ambushing, the team were always wary of them. They had been on the Japanese side until they realised that wasn't working for them and switched sides and the team didn't have complete trust in them. But with the numbers they had, they hoped to be able to do great work. The team also found a Japanese transit camp on the way to Moulmein, and called in an airstrike which was successful. While they knew the Japanese were clearly close, they felt relatively safe in their jungle camp, Fred said they might have only been a few miles from the enemy but in the jungle it could have been 30 miles. In the days following the airstrike they heard from locals that there were Indian soldiers in the area and they duly found the camp with their guide. It turned out they had been captured but had managed to escape, and were in a poor state having been almost starved until they agreed to fight for the Japanese. Of course once allowed out to fight they escaped but were scared of repercussions, fearful that having fought alongside the Japanese, albeit reluctantly, they might lose their pensions and be left destitute. Fred clearly felt for these men and the team were pleased to have them join them and swell their force. Fred said they were quite a motley crew, British, Burmese levies, Indians along with what they felt were the unreliable BNA soldiers.

---

73 National Archive, HS1

Fred around the age of 1 in his beloved Eastbourne

Fred at school

Fred and family back in Eastbourne

Fred at his sister's wedding, far right

Team Citroen in Algeria

TO ALL WHOM IT MAY CONCERN:

The bearer is a fully accredited representative of the Supreme Allied High Command. He has been instructed to join forces wherever possible with resistance units to wage unceasing war against the German invader for the liberation of FRANCE.

Le militaire porteur de la présente est le représentant pleinement accrédité du Commandement Suprême Interallié. Il a reçu pour instructions de se joindre partout où cela sera possible aux groupes de résistance pour poursuivre à leurs côtés contre l'envahisseur allemand une lutte qui ne doit cesser qu'avec la libération du territoire français.

(Signature du porteur) ....

Pour le Général Sir Henry Maitland Wilson,
Commandant Suprême pour le Théâtre
d'Opérations de la Méditerranée,
et par son ordre :

Signé : ....

Commandant en Chef, Forces Françaises
de l'Intérieur, Zone Sud.

The card Fred carried on him in France, explaining his role

Fred outside the Hotel Crillon, Avignon

Fred wearing the beret badge that causes much discussion

Fred and team in Italy

Fred and team in Egypt

Sergeant's Mess, Hondona

At the Saw Bali Camp, Burma

In Burma with one of the elephants, Fred riding on the right

The team receiving a drop in Burma

Fred and friends at Mount Lavinia Hotel

Fred and fellow Jeds enjoying a game of tennis, Ceylon

Fred and fellow Jeds at Bentota beach

Fred, Tom Henny and another with the car they stole in Kuala Lumpur, 1945

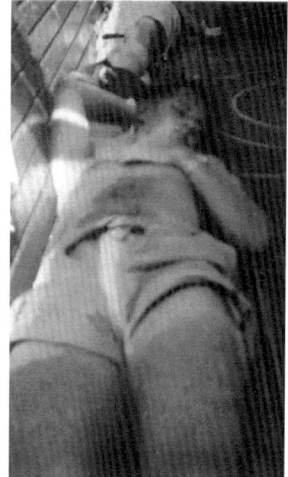

Fred on deck, heading home from India in 1946

Fred and Sylvia's wedding, 1951

Fred with colleagues in his early days at Portsmouth Water Company

Fred and Sheila's wedding, 1976

Fred on his 60th Birthday with his neighbour retired Commander Hal Eddows in the background

The reunion in Paris, at Mount Valerian, 1984

Fred and Jed friends in Washington for the American reunion, 1987

Fred and friends arriving in Northern France for the 50th anniversary of D-Day

Reunion at the *Cutty Sark*, photo courtesy of Simon Leney

Reunion at Arundel over a few days, not all who attended in photo, Fred on far right

Fred installed as President of Portsmouth and Southsea Rotary Club

Pushing the grandchildren up his beloved garden in the early 1990s

Fred and Sheila at one of the many social events they attended

Meeting Princess Anne at the Natural History Museum, Photo courtesy of Simon and Kay DeHalpert

Receiving the Legion d'Honneur at the D-Day Museum in Portsmouth, 2016

Fred's first attendance at the Cenotaph Parade, 2016

Fred with his son, John and daughter, Judith at the unveiling of the Lysander replica at Tangmere Military Aviation Museum

Fred with the McGregor brothers filming for *RAF at 100*

Fred with contestants from *Secret Agent Selection and* others at Tangmere Military Aviation Museum

Fred again accompanied by his son, John, at the Cenotaph Remembrance Service, 2018

Fred

Fred on his last birthday, age 99

Inevitably this continual routine of successful ambushing was beginning to attract attention and the airstrike proved the final straw for the Japanese. During the night of 23 May a group of 46 Japanese attacked the camp. However, initially unknown to the team, they were part of a 600 strong force who had arrived in the area to clear it of the BNA and they were also aware of a covert group operating in the area. The airdrops of supplies were clearly visible to the enemy troops.

The Japanese attacked from the north of the camp, which housed the BNA contingent. One of the team's levies was leaving the camp when the enemy arrived. He grabbed a Bren gun from the sentry and opened fire, killing several Japanese. The Japanese replied with both rifle fire and grenades and the BNA contingent fled to high ground south of the camp. The single levy, with no support, withdrew. At the moment this was happening news came through of the arrival of 600 Japanese troops and it was assumed they were attempting to surround the camp, so the teams withdrew. As a precaution the teams had already secreted spare food and wireless equipment as well as other items in a cave near Minlwin in case of such an emergency. Fred said they had little time to grab essentials, his priority was the radio, code books and spare batteries. They hid the radio set they were using, grabbed an emergency supply of food and moved towards Natgyo. From this point it was Teams Cow and Giraffe with just 6 levies moving through the jungle. They managed to avoid a Japanese patrol of 20 men by mere seconds, which was moving from Mygaungeing to Chauknkwa. They stayed hidden in the jungle all day, moving at dusk to Natgyo where they met up with another 10 levies, Fred recalled they hid out on a hill and due to the thick jungle could sit and watch the camp. While sitting in the jungle Fred had the horrible realisation that he had neither taken the steam generator or hidden it. They found out that the Japanese had only gone halfway into the camp, destroying the huts used by the BNA, so the decision to return to the camp was taken. The risk of capture versus regaining equipment and supplies was deemed worthwhile. Fred recalled returning to the camp with just a guide, he always said that walking through the jungle in the dark with just one guide and going back into the camp was a frightening experience. The steam generator was nowhere to be found, having either been destroyed or lost within the camp or the Japanese had taken it away. The official report suggests it was hidden; whether this was an attempt to hide the fact the team had lost it or whether they thought it might be found later is unclear. They were able to move and find a safe place to sleep for a few hours, Fred then sent an uncoded message 'send Jenny', which alerted HQ that they needed a new steam generator; he was worried that if the batteries died they would have no way of communicating. They then moved through the jungle finding another location for a night. During this time radio contact was made with Calcutta twice.

The following day a small party returned again to the camp to retrieve more food that had been hidden in the area but left when they mistook INA troops for Japanese. These troops had dispersed during the attack on the camp but had returned to look for the British teams.

They had thought that they would be able to simply locate their camp a little further away, but it quickly became apparent that the Japanese were not going to give up and in Fred's words chased them 'from arsehole to breakfast time for six weeks'.[74] This phrase was used in an interview and was one he never used with the family, his language could be colourful if in the company of men, but was unfailingly polite if women were present - a true gent.

They moved through the jungle at dusk, having received a report, which turned out to be inaccurate, that the 14th Army was approaching Bilin. The teams, now with the Indian troops decided to stay there for the day, but rather than friendly troops approaching, 300 enemy troops arrived just down the road at Wiyaw with intelligence suggesting they would start searching the mountain area the next day. Yet again they set off through the jungle, the teams were careful not to disclose information to the INA (Indian National Army) troops, they are described as a millstone around the neck of the teams, this in spite of the positive view that Fred had of them. Nonetheless, they felt unable to abandon them and risk their capture by the Japanese, they knew too much about the teams. Notwithstanding, the terrain was very challenging and along the way they lost contact with 13 of the INA and they were left behind as it was simply too dangerous to return and search for them. They were all very aware of being, in the report's words, trailed by the Japanese throughout this time. Fred used the word chased, which seems more accurate in terms of what they were clearly feeling. He said they slept in a different place every night, at each village they would pick up a new guide to take them on further. The guides were quite limited in their knowledge, they could take them to the next village but then they would need another guide to get them to the next. Fred said they were always on the lookout for good guides, to help them through the thick jungle. They lost the contingent of BNA, who simply melted away, so their group was much reduced. He said the relentless chase was exhausting and frustrating;

---

74 Sean Rayment, *Tales from the Special Forces Club*, p.253

they wanted to get back to their main role but instead were basically on the run. They slept in the soft mud often with rain falling on them during this time, Fred said the villagers that they encountered were friendly, happy to provide a guide and food for them. He felt that this was, in part, due to the brutality that the Japanese were dishing out. Fred often said had the Japanese been kinder, the villagers may not have afforded the team so much assistance. It was during this incessant chase that the team bought two elephants. The only issue being that they really couldn't carry more than a mule and the seller had not warned them that elephants need a day of rest every three days. Needless to say the endless marching did not go down well with the elephants, who decided one night they had had enough and wandered off into the jungle never to be seen again. This was clearly a light moment, although it must have been frustrating, during what was a pretty horrific experience. It was the one story that Fred used to enjoy telling, laughing almost till he cried. It was a story we all enjoyed hearing and one that very firmly stuck in the memory for his grandchildren.

Fred recalled that the team and its assorted group tried to circle back towards the main road so that they could continue with their work, hacking through jungle, dealing with the heat, leeches and other assorted difficulties. After a few weeks they were back to the main road which was a significant transit route for the enemy. Having had some supply drops the Indian troops were now armed with Sten guns, Fred and the team had their favoured US carbines. They also had Mills grenades and a PIAT, which was a hand-held anti-tank weapon. The PIAT had a range of around 100 yards and the team set up to ambush a convoy. Unfortunately, the PIAT proved unreliable in its aim and two attempts both missed, which was frustrating as they were only about 20 yards away. Fred would say it knocked your shoulder out of its joint every time you used it. Naturally the convoy stopped and in Fred's words 'a ferocious firefight' ensued, the Allies enjoying the upper hand for a short while before the Japanese started to organise themselves, at which point the team melted back into the jungle, realising they could do no more damage. Fred said they were often substantially outnumbered when they did engage, so they tended to attempt to attack smaller convoys where they felt they had a chance.

The official report details that the Japanese tortured villagers to gather information on the teams and that reprisals were carried out. Fred recalled this with obvious upset, stating he had never seen such cruelty. He often said the reprisals he saw in France against the collaborators were nothing compared to what happened in the jungle. One village the teams had passed through was burnt to the ground with 18 Karens thrown into a well and shot, with just 3 rescued, and another two villages were partially burnt down. Fred commented on the number of women, including elderly women, raped in these villages, decades later you could still see the fury and upset in his eyes. In Minlwin a large number of the villagers were tortured and ten levies were taken from this village, their fate unknown. The Japanese, at this village, also had a list of all the men in the village that had been supplied with weapons. Beyond that they knew all details of supply drops and the make-up of the teams. They were clearly very determined to find and eradicate the teams and all who they assisted. This was a treacherous and very dangerous time for Fred and his colleagues.

It seems that around Naungadok the Japanese took a break from chasing the team, and on 28 May they were able to set up a temporary camp. They all needed a slight break from the constant strain of trekking through the jungle, they had been surviving on a handful of unpolished rice a day and were all beginning to suffer. Fred recalled three straight days of this unpolished rice and of being really sick. He said their physical health deteriorated rapidly from being very fit to beginning to starve. During this arduous period Fred remembered one day sitting on a log when an enormous spider crawled out from it. It was so large that they had no option but to shoot it, after which they decided to burn the log and as they did so hundreds of baby spiders ran from it and scurried away. It's always interesting when looking at this period that Fred and other Jeds seemed to treat it as a bit of an adventure. While it was adventurous, their ability to reflect in a positive and at times very humorous way is so informative to the character of these men. While shooting a large spider might appear excessive, it gives a hint of what they were facing. At a time when they wouldn't have wanted to give a hint of their location, they shot a spider. The jungle may have masked them quite well but it worked both ways, hiding the enemy as well.

They urgently needed food and Calcutta arranged a drop on 1 June and on the 4th they received a new steam generator which had been requested as they moved through the jungle. Fred had also been very relieved that base had understood his 'send Jenny' message and he was able to communicate with base. They had also managed to borrow a battery from Colonel Critchley of Mongoose; one of their runners had gone for food in the Leke area and managed to secure the battery as well. Inevitably the two drops were seen by the Japanese and the chase resumed.

They moved on and were able to secure another drop on 6 June which included food, clothing as well as some ammunition. The Japanese arrived close by on the 8th and the team moved up into hills grabbing as many stores as they could and burning what was left. The next morning 100 Japanese entered the camp they had abandoned. It's impossible to understand the unrelenting pressure on the teams, the jungle, the lack of food and the immediate knowledge that those chasing you were not far behind. They were able on 9 June to contact a commander in the BNA, Bo Hon Shwe who reported that he had 20 men with him but many more were scattered throughout the area.

Throughout this time, McAdam from Team Giraffe had been elsewhere, he had gone on a recce on the night the camp was attacked. He had heard of the attack and decided to stay with Z Force whom he had met with. Due to the ability of Fred and no doubt the Giraffe radio operator, Sgt Edgar, McAdam was able to get information on Cow and Giraffe via Calcutta using Z Force's radio, but attempts to send runners to locate them proved impossible. He reports on the intensity of the presence of the Japanese troops and their occupation of many villages as well as their holding the roads.

In spite this, McAdam reported on several successful ambushes, one involved a group of BNA with just one Sten gun who had fashioned spears from bamboos with sharp points. They ambushed 6 Japanese officers killing five and collecting what was referred to as booty which included 5 swords. Another group managed to ambush a car on the road east from Thaton. The RAF had also bombed in the area, and a BNA group were able to enter Wutgyi afterwards and capture food and clothing left behind by the fleeing Japanese. When asked about the heat and sun, Fred would say that the only protection for his skin was to get a tan. Unfortunately in later years this would come back to bite him with multiple basal cell carcinomas and a squamous cell carcinoma, all of which were treated.

Through information from Calcutta and runners who were scouting the area, McAdam got a fix on Cow and Giraffe on 5 June and intended to head back to them. Unfortunately, word came through that once again they were on the run, being chased mercilessly. McAdam was instructed to stay with Z Force until otherwise instructed. The next day Z Force were instructed to move north towards the Mongoose area, this team was finishing up and preparing to evacuate. After 3 days of moving north on 10 June they sent a runner to make contact with a British officer who was reported to be at Kyowaing, he gained information that British officers were in the area so returned the next morning. On this occasion he ran into another levy from Major Ford of

Mongoose's team, who he found at Ta-Ukyi. Colonel Critchley arrived at this village the next day and signalled McCoull to bring Cow and Giraffe to Kyowaing as soon as they could. McAdam and Critchley moved to Kyowaing on 13 June, and finally McAdam was reunited with his team on the 14th.

A meeting between McCoull, McAdam and Critchley discussed the issues for the team in the area. These rested on the inability of the allies to cross the Sittang River, which allowed the Japanese the time to reorganise and reassert themselves. It was very clear that if the teams continued to engage, even if they could, the area was deemed unsuited to guerrilla warfare, the ground was flat and given the strength of the enemy forces, there was no room for manoeuvre in the region. They also realised that with the Japanese holding a strong presence in the area the reprisals of rape and murder would continue to rain down on the locals if any activity continued. As Teams Cow and Giraffe had been forced north towards Mongoose territory and the coming monsoon which would see Mongoose cutting down their activities it was decided that Cow and Giraffe would be evacuated. Their position was simply too precarious, in the midst of the Japanese, while on retreat in many areas, this did not reduce their potency or the brutality of the fight either against the British or the local population. They had spent six weeks in the jungle, during which they had been successful in ambushing and distracting the enemy.

Ultimately, they managed to get to an airstrip run by Major Trofimov at Kyowaing and escaped, but it had to be a fast turnaround. Apparently three aircraft arrived, one took Team Cow, another Team Giraffe, the third aircraft took, Major Ronnie Kaulbeck.[75] Official records make little mention of the team's evacuation other than stating they left on 17 June. Fred though was happy to discuss this particular event as it left a lifelong impression on him.

Team Cow along with one Burmese guide bundled themselves into a Lysander on 17 June 1945 and were whisked to safety. Fred said he saw nothing of the flight as his face was pressed to the floor of the aircraft with the other two team members on top of him. He said the Burmese guide had jumped in with the pilot up front. What the pilot must have made of this motley group, five men in a two-seater aircraft, who knows, but Fred was certainly pleased to be flown out

---

75   A A E Trofimov, *A Most Irregular War*, Bcester: evon Press & The Trofimov Literary Estate, 2023, p.139

of the jungle. While 5 men in a Lysander was not normal, when it came to the Jeds it was not entirely unknown and other reports exist of several men and even a dog in the back of this workhorse of an aircraft escaping from various locations. Initially flown to Rangoon, from there on 21 June, Fred and another four Jeds sailed on an old boat back to Calcutta. Fred recalled that an Indian soldier was stabbed by another, he commented that the Jeds made sure they steered clear of others on the boat and kept to themselves. After this it was another 5 days on a train to Ceylon and on to the training site at Hondona, where Fred had what he referred to as a short break.

Fred was one of many Jeds who volunteered for the Far East. While he was part of Operation Nation, Operation Character, also in Burma, also had a number of Jeds known to Fred. One friend of Fred's, Roger Leney, who had been instrumental in getting Fred out of Italy, wrote in great detail about his experiences in Burma. Roger had gone in before Fred and like Fred his team got themselves elephants, he mentions his boots disintegrating during the monsoon as well as sweat bees who stung his armpits.[76] One humorous moment was when he and others dived for cover, thinking they could hear nearby machine guns only for the locals to laugh and tell them it was woodpeckers. Roger, at one point, had to leave the jungle for Rangoon to get treatment, his lack of good footwear causing an infection.

John Sharpe, another of Fred's friends from those far off days at Bovington and Scarborough also found himself in the Far East. He was part of Team Camel with Major Tom Carew and Captain J Cox. His first mission resulted in them being brought out after two months as they were given chase much like Fred's team. However, they got a second opportunity and worked with Karen tribesmen, who had suffered terrible brutality from the Japanese. John Sharpe said the jungle aged him, malaria and dysentery, he said once you were ill you stayed ill.[77] The Character operation focused on the area where the Karens were situated, these were a loyal group and reliable, as Major Seagram had previously found. Nonetheless, the teams witnessed terrible events on both sides.

Beyond the British Jeds, many American Jeds including Jack Singlaub joined the OSS in the Far East and saw action. There were also French Jeds who went to French Indo-China.

---

76 Roger Leney, unpublished memoirs, courtesy of Simon Leney
77 Sean Rayment, *Tales from the Special Forces Club*, p.304

One lasting effect of Fred's time in the Far East was his steadfast refusal to ever eat corned beef. Tins of corned beef were included in their supply drops, but the heat ensured that the beef was liquid and simply poured out of the tins. But even supply drops became impossible and after so many weeks of relentless escape from the enemy, living on barely anything, the daily handful of rice even running out. Fred would, when recalling the jungle, regularly refer to the black rice, which was quite fibrous but gave them diarrhoea. Fred oftentimes reflected on that radio message declaring Victory in Europe and the instruction to celebrate. While it had come in during those early weeks, in later years he regarded the message as almost offensive, rather than the morale boost it was perhaps intended to be. Jeds throughout the region were scrambling to stay alive, being hunted day and night, starving and seeing the horrors the Japanese were inflicting on the population, women raped, murders, even killing animals so that those left would likely starve, no - celebrating victory in Europe had not been something they were inclined to indulge in.

The Nation operation, of which Team Cow was part, listed 3,381 Japanese killed, with 201 injured and 156 taken as prisoners of war. The allies listed 13 killed and 52 injured. As in France, The Jedburghs proved their worth and while suffering losses, they were far less than those inflicted on the enemy.

Given the horrors Fred witnessed during this period, for the rest of his life he chose to focus on the good that he did, offering aid and assistance where he could and often telling the story of the elephants, 'disappearing into the night'. He laughed off much of his experience, finding a grim humour in his loathing of corned beef and enormous spiders. He shrugged off the skin cancers in later years as a price he had to pay.

There is discussion around the impact of Force 136 after the war, with issues around the supply of arms to the BNA and the controversy of some Force 136 members returning to Burma to fight with the Karen people against the Burmese government but for the purposes of this work, it is worth simply noting that the Jedburgh men volunteered and did all they could to defeat a brutal force. Fred and his team were not the only ones to suffer deprivations, yet all the Jedburghs reflected positively on their work in the Far East. Fred felt they made a difference, whether it was ambushing the enemy, or assisting the locals both by arming and training them but also by providing medical help. He always said they went into Burma in good time, time to actually do something. The fact that they kept a significant number of Japanese involved in simply chasing them meant that other plans were thwarted.

The brutality meted out to locals by the Japanese for helping the teams was certainly a weight that stayed with Fred, but he needed for his own sanity to reflect on the positive.

For Fred though this wasn't the end of the war, not just yet. He still had more to do and was keen as mustard to do one more job.

After Burma and the experiences there, no-one would have blamed Fred if he had had enough and wanted to head home. Yet after what Fred called a short break at Hondona, it was from here that Fred then moved on to Malaya to rescue shot-down American airmen.

The situation in Malaya was complex, initially the Malay had accepted the Japanese with an inevitability and the Japanese maintained their demeanour of benevolent occupiers releasing the country from imperial control. However, the mask, as in Burma, soon slipped. Instances began with minor face slaps but progressed to torture; the Malay still feared the Japanese, but hated them. As in Burma, they wanted to be free of imperial rule and simply swapping one for another was not an option. Nonetheless there were some who joined with the British to aid in the defeat of the Japanese.

The Malaya peninsula was around 700 miles by 250 miles and when the Japanese invaded only about a fifth was inhabited. Much was forest, jungle or mangrove but the Japanese attempted to start clearing land to make room for rice fields.[78] Towns and harbours of any significance were situated in coastal areas. Outside Singapore, Penang and Malacca, other territories had accepted British advisors but not rule. The population across the region was a mix of Malay, Chinese and Indian. The native Malay tended to be more rural and worked in the limited agricultural sector. The Chinese, who outnumbered the Malay in several areas, centred themselves in towns and seemed to have more control over the wealth and economy. This added to the complexity of the situation. The early years of the war had provided challenges in getting people and arms onto the Malay peninsula, submarines being used multiple times. However, the transfer from submarine to boat to shore was fraught with difficulties. Additionally, personnel and equipment then had arduous journeys into the hills to reach areas suitable for a resistance to hide. It would be November 1944 before a squadron of Liberators was made available. These aircraft made an enormous difference to the range of operations possible. There were still issues, requests for air reconnaissance were refused due to

---

78 National Archive File

distance, so determining drop zones was almost impossible and some areas were still outside the range of the aircraft which were based in Jessore. Drop zones were chosen from maps and the hopefully reliable knowledge of officers being dropped to the region.

When it became clear that the Japanese were going to surrender, questions abounded about the fate for those resisters and those who had initially supported the Japanese, a directive from Mountbatten suggesting that troops were not to engage in discussions and gives clear instructions as to what to say to various groups.

Fred had been on his short break for some time, around five weeks, but on 8th August 1945 Fred was dropped into Malaya under the Guitar Signal Plan, just a week before what would come to be known as VJ Day on 15 August. Dates are less settled though; it seems on 11 August surrender was clearly coming but it was 17 August before the ceasefire order was sent out. No-one knew how the Japanese troops in Malaya would react, instructions were to avoid areas where Japanese were still situated.

In the midst of this fast changing landscape Fred dropped with Captain A R G Morrison, codename Apple and Sergeant B C Lee, code name Pear, who is listed as a coder, they were listed as attached to G.L.O. Selangor. Fruits, vegetables and garden implements seem to have been the choice for code names in this particular theatre. Fred was one of 46 wireless operators in Malaya during this time along with 88 British officers.

Also dropped were Sergeant Eldridge and Sergeant Wong to drop zone Ulu Yam. Fred's code name was Plum on this occasion and various reports refer to the team as Team Surrey. Reports on their landing specify they were dropped from a 'phenomenal height' estimated at 1100-1200 feet, Fred would no doubt have not been surprised but disappointed at another unnecessarily high drop. They landed in broad daylight at 5.30 in the afternoon, which would have heightened the risks of being spotted. Apparently one of the men landed on the outskirts of a village with 50 Japanese troops in it, but luckily for whatever reason the Japanese did nothing at this point. The supplies were also dropped from too high and were spread across the local village, far from ideal. Those on the ground reported that another drop to nearby Rusa was high and would have been visible to the enemy. Fred landed into the Selangor region under Operation Galvanic. This operation had been introduced into the Selangor area in early June 1945. Due to enemy activity patrols were restricted but a good amount of information relating to road and rail traffic was obtained. This was valuable as the areas covered were just to the north of the beachhead for the proposed landings of liberating forces. Official records refer to the Japanese occupation as uncouth, which would seem to be a wonderfully understated comment but typical of the language often found in files from the period.

The day after landing Fred along with Captain Morrison and Sergeant Lee left Ulu Yam for Rusa to collect supplies and then move onto the Serendah camp. The team had dropped into a difficult area, it was reported that those on the ground were suffering difficulties with food supplies and living on rice and roots, it was reported that while the food situation was not desperate it was 'somewhat tight'. Given Fred's experiences in Burma this may not have fazed him as he rarely spoke in detail about this. The following day around 200 enemy troops descended on the Ulu Yam drop zone to search it, apparently coming from the Serendah drop zone area, so it was a very active area. The team, were attached to Orange Patrol which consisted of Major Thomson-Walker of the Royal Engineers, Squadron Leader Robertson of the Royal Australian Air Force, Sergeant D J Richardson of the Royal Gloucestershire Huzzars. Richardson, had sadly been killed, with Sergeant Elvidge from the Royal Corps of Signals, who dropped in with Fred to replace Sergeant Richardson. The team also had Seah Tin Toon a Chinese interpreter and Sergeant Wong of the Canadian Infantry Corps who was also listed as an interpreter and who also dropped in with Fred. This Orange Patrol are listed as having a fighting force of 94, they were the 1st group of multiple groups in various areas, according to an official report in August 1945.[79] Major Thomson-Walker in his report states that the news of the imminent Japanese surrender was received on 11 August but in his words, 'did not feel very true'.

In interviews Fred confirmed that their role was to retrieve downed airmen. This was no doubt a different operation due to the changing landscape as plans show the Jeds were originally going to be used in their more traditional role during a retaking of the region. It's not clear how many, if any, airmen were found and delivered back to safety but there were hazards. Despite dropping in so close to the end of the war, many Japanese soldiers were unaware that their country had surrendered so even after the official end of the war there was jeopardy.

Fred often recalled one particular incident. A few weeks after his arrival and the official end of the war, his team was attacked by some Japanese troops. Approximately 90 Japanese attacked the village they were in. Fred said they were in Serandah. It was unprovoked and

---

79 National Archives File

indeed they had been aware of Japanese troops passing nearby, who seemed to have no interest by this stage of engaging with their former foes.[80] Yet on 31 August they did, a sentry had stumbled across the enemy and a firefight ensued, the sentry was killed. Fred said the team found themselves pinned in the village police station taking heavy fire. They were fast running out of ammunition and Fred felt his time may well have been up at this point; it was relentless and was the one time Fred truly felt that he may not get out alive. Fortunately a British officer with a group of about a dozen Ghurkas were nearby. Fred said they were at a hospital and heard the commotion and arrived, waving a Union Jack, just in time. Fred always said that was the closest call he had and official records comment that it defeated comprehension as to how they were not wiped out. He always held the Gurkhas in the highest esteem as he credited them with saving his life. This all happened after the official end of the war, so while celebrations were ongoing elsewhere, Fred and many others were still risking their lives and simply hoping for the day they could head home.

Fred said he was one of the first British men into Kuala Lumpur and talked of the Japanese walking around, all with their rifles and bayonets still attached. While Chinese guerrillas had entered Kuala Lumpur with them, they had to wait for more British troops to emerge from the jungle. Fred felt that with the force they had, they could have quelled the insurrection that took place. He felt they could have disarmed them all without any near the amount of trouble that did ensue. Whether this was feasible we shall never know, but a Jed always thought positively and had a skill set beyond the norm.

Fred left Kuala Lumpur with a group of guerrillas for Kajang. Fred realised there was trouble brewing. There was a lot of political jargon being spoken by varying communist groups and they were being listened to. He said he reported this back to John Davis in Kuala Lumpur, but that he was very loyal to the Chinese guerillas – just as they were loyal to him, according to Fred. As such he would not hear of a word against them. Fred said this was the start of the troubles and Kajang was the centre of it.[81]

Official reports show that Fred arrived in Malaya too late to carry out his normal duties, he is shown as the second wireless operator within the Orange Patrol, but the report also states that he worked well

---

80 Personal comms
81 Post-war issues and political issues would rage in Malaya for years.

on other jobs assigned to him. The sudden end of the war had altered Fred's role but one suspects he did not mind.

Some of Fred's reticence in talking about his experiences can perhaps be found in the various pieces of paperwork which litter the archives. In the case of Force 136, it states that they may discuss being despatched by parachute, raising guerrillas and fostering resistance but is clear that technical issues cannot be discussed and neither can details of any locals who worked with them. Fred, like all the Jeds, took their signing of the official secrets act very seriously and in spite of being told that they could discuss their war years maintained a discretion which now with them all gone means that we can only piece together certain segments and draw our own conclusions based on what they did say and what the records say. The hardships encountered by Fred and other Jeds are often focused on and rightly so; they suffered enormous physical deprivations and the demands on their bodies of marching through the jungle is unimaginable for most of us. Decades later the sun shining on Fred during this time caused multiple skin cancers; the war never quite left him. Yet, and this is a mark of the Jeds, this odd bunch, endured with humour. One story tells of an NCO barely able to walk with all he was carrying asking for more to carry otherwise he might break into a gallop. This self effacing attitude seems to have been rampant among the Jeds, along with humour in the face of adversity. Another who commented on those good days in the jungle was reminded that his back was raw from carrying his equipment and that his team had to dress his wounds, his reaction 'I had forgotten that'. Despite the hardships endured, there remained a strong camaraderie and the men who came home chose to focus on that rather than the horrors they had borne witness to.

There were moments, of course, in Ceylon, during acclimatisation or between operations, when a bit of R and R was enjoyed. There are reports of raucous evenings in the NCOs' mess, where copious amounts of alcohol were consumed most nights. The men providing their own entertainment from jokes to singing, with various individuals having to be carried back to their bunks at the end of the evening's revelry. Fred was a great pianist and while unable to read music, he could simply hear a tune and then play it. He would have been a popular turn at these evenings.

Fred would look at photos which show him with colleagues at the Mount Lavinia Hotel at Colombo Beach, he would smile wistfully and say, 'that's where we did our courting'. Ever the gentleman, that's as much information as he would divulge, but the smile and twinkle in his eye said it all. Clearly the female company was welcome and much enjoyed. It was a popular spot for afternoon tea on the terrace with several Jeds mentioning it. The hotel still exists today and the structure is little changed, its location spectacular, and one can imagine Fred and others taking tea on the terrace, enjoying looking out to sea wondering when they might get home. Trips to the beach at Bentota were clearly enjoyed and we have several photos of Fred and his friends enjoying the water and the very hot sand. It was apparently almost a sport watching new arrivals attempt the dash down the beach to the water, many turned back to retrieve footwear and those who made it to the water had to endure the raucous banter should they ask for their footwear to be brought to the water's edge, yet multiple photos show many of them relaxing on the sand at the water's edge. The exotic nature of the locations, palm trees, the heat, afternoon tea on the hotel terrace were all welcome distractions and temporary relief from jungle warfare or the thought of it. Harry Verlander mentions sending tea home to his mother, yet Fred never commented on these brief moments of rest other than to smile at the memory of the Mount Lavinia Hotel.

The post-war situation in Burma and Malaya would prove even more complex. Burma gained independence in 1948 but was plagued by instability based around the various ethnic groups and the military. In Malaya, the Malayan Union was formed in 1946, followed by the Federation of Malaya in 1948, but unrest continued with independence being granted in 1957. It was renamed Malaysia in 1963 when the territories of Singapore, Sarawak and North Borneo joined.

Fred returned to Britain on his birthday, in 1946, to a country changed, having spent some time in India, which he never discussed. He was 23 years old on that day and had experienced so much since signing up on his 18th birthday, full of enthusiasm and ready to serve his country. If asked about his service he would simply say it was secret and that was the end of the conversation. Everyone who lived through the war understood the privations and no-one wanted to intrude into another's life looking for details. It was in the past and that was where people wanted it to stay. Fred, in particular, seems to have been happy to leave it behind. Unlike some he did not keep any mementos of his time serving, save for some photographs and at one time he had a silk handkerchief. His memories were more than enough for him.

CHAPTER FIVE

POST WAR – PERSONAL LIFE

Having arrived back on his birthday, 20 November 1946, we're not sure if there was a family celebration but one would have hoped so, although it is thought not. He always said he felt his parents were proud of him but they were of a generation which expressed little overt affection. Yet, there had been an article in their local *Observer* newspaper, in 1946, detailing Fred being award the Croix de Guerre along with a photo. It specifies that he was awarded the medal for gallantry in France in August 1944 and mentioned in despatches, it says, for gallantry in Malaya. It states that he was in the Special Airborne Force, which is perhaps as close as his parents could be told, and also perhaps gives a hint of what Fred and others were able to tell their families. It mentions that he was dropped into France and Rangoon and had been in the thick of the fighting in multiple areas, although not all were correct. At the time of the newspaper report, he was in India awaiting demob and a return home. For that reason the Croix de Guerre was posted to him. His mother said she hoped to have him home for Christmas, which she did. She gave the interesting information that while Fred was not able to send letters while on active service, she apparently received a monthly update from a First Aid Nursing Yeomanry officer so knew he was at least alive. The fact that his parents contacted the local paper shows that they were enormously proud, even though they knew almost nothing of his wartime service.[82] Having been kept informed that he was safe throughout his service, they understood he was involved in something both secret and special, but never enquired. It's impossible for others to speculate as to what it was like for those men returning home, those who served in the Jedburghs were very specifically chosen and to that

---

82 Family papers, cut out from the *Observer* but date unknown.

end many, like Fred, were able to put the war behind them and get on with their lives. Fred kept the newspaper cutting all his life, no doubt honoured that his local paper had acknowledged his contribution and perhaps got a sense of pride from his parents.

By this point SOE had been wound up but in spite of the absolute secrecy, a film, *Now It Can Be Told*, was made.[83] It employed real agents and attempted to tell something of the story of the clandestine work that was done. It seems to have fallen from view, but remains available and more recently Martyn Cox has worked on reviving sections and making it accessible to the modern audience, who prefer bite-sized information.

Fred, without doubt, was delighted to get home and returned to work at the Colne Valley Water Company. It really was a case of picking up the threads of his previous life and carrying on as if nothing had happened. One thing that Fred lobbied for, while at Colne Valley, was the laying of water pipes alongside the new M1 motorway that was completed in 1959. He argued that it would allow water to be transported from one part of the country to another in the event of a drought. His idea was deemed unnecessary; he was always slightly irritated by the fact that those above him thought they knew better and felt the idea of a water shortage anywhere in the country ridiculous. Of course, time has shown that it would likely have been a good idea. In 1951 he married his first wife Sylvia at Westminster Register Office. They had met and fallen in love while both working at the water company. They had no children although Sylvia did sadly suffer a number of miscarriages.

In 1962 Fred and Sylvia moved to Portsmouth, with Fred taking up a position as Assistant Secretary at the Portsmouth Water Company. When he attended the interview for the job, he had been shocked to find he was being interviewed by the entire board of nine men. While he was delighted to get the job, he was a bit annoyed at being asked to qualify as an accountant. He had thought his qualification as a Chartered Company Secretary would be enough, but he complied and duly added to his qualifications. The company, established in 1857, was in a period of growth, the mid 1950s had seen it double its size by the amalgamation with the nearby Gosport Waterworks Company. In Fred's first year they again doubled their area with four acquisitions in West Sussex. The company would move from Portsmouth to nearby Havant in 1967. He and Sylvia had a few homes in the area

---

83   Dir. Teddy Baird, *Now It Can Be Told*, 1947

before settling in Bosham, near Chichester, in 1971 where Fred would remain for the rest of his life. A quiet, unassuming village when Fred moved there, it belied its history. The birth and burial place of the last Saxon Kings and even King Canute. It was the harbour from which King Harold sailed to France in 1064 and is depicted in the Bayeaux Tapestry. While it remains a lovely village, it has attracted a large influx of people, particularly from London, looking for the quintessential English village and attracts large numbers of visitors, especially in the summer. It was a village that Fred loved and it is his final resting place.

In 1974, the former Secretary and Treasurer of the company retired and Fred took up the post. In the previous year, the government had put pressure on water companies to provide pension schemes for all employees. The Portsmouth Water Company had been providing this since 1925 and took what would be, a significant decision to keep this scheme in place for existing employees.

Sylvia had suffered from ill health for some years and passed away quite suddenly in January 1976. Despite being married for a quarter of a century, Fred never spoke of Sylvia in any detail. Fred was always reluctant to discuss the personal side of this period and we only know a few pieces of information. It was clearly his way of dealing with difficult or sad situations and times, leave them in the past. While Fred always refused to engage in any betting or going to the races, which we thought was rooted in his experience at Monopoli, we do have a photo of Fred with Sylvia at the races. It may have been this was something they did and when she died, he simply closed the door on that.

After Sylvia's death, one of the accounts staff at the water company, Sheila, invited him to Sunday tea. Having been widowed herself some years before, she knew how difficult it could be to find yourself alone. She was encouraged to invite Fred by her daughter, but hesitated for several weeks as Fred was the boss and she wasn't at all sure how he would receive an invitation to tea. He had always been particularly kind to Sheila, dropping bags of apples and other produce from his garden into the office for her. Her children fondly remember the water company Christmas parties and Judith, being a bit older than her brother, said Fred always said hello and had a kindly word. He was aware of her situation, a widow having to work full time to provide for her family. As it turned out Fred was delighted to be invited, and duly arrived one Sunday afternoon armed with a cake mix, some chocolates and dog biscuits. It seems he had raided his larder, realising he should not arrive empty handed. Fortunately for Fred, Sheila was a great baker and also had a dog, so the gifts were well received and no one goes wrong with chocolates. They hit it off immediately and unexpectedly for both of them a romance blossomed. While Sheila's daughter was 21, her son at 13 found the incursion of a new man more difficult to negotiate. Suddenly here was someone new, telling him how to hold his cup and checking his homework. John's early memories of Fred show how both found it a challenge to adapt to a new family dynamic. Nevertheless, John was pleased to see his mother happy following the difficulties of being a widowed mother in the late 1960s and early 1970s.

Fred married Sheila in November 1976, with John giving his mother away, to the delight of their friends and family. From comments Sheila made on their 25th anniversary, it's clear that the speed of their relationship and marriage caused a few raised eyebrows. Sheila had been widowed for seven years and was a strict Catholic, while Fred was ever the gentleman, so while it was undoubtedly a speedy courtship and marriage there was no scandal hiding in the wings. Clearly neither of them wanted to waste a moment of whatever time they might have together. Sheila with her adult daughter and teenage son had moved to Bosham around Easter at Fred's invitation and Fred found himself with a ready-made family. They also brought their beloved dog, Patch, who Fred took to immediately. He had owned several dogs over the years and Patch would find the new man in his family's life a man who spoiled him rotten. So much so that Patch would refuse a Bonio biscuit unless it was slathered in butter with bacon on top. Fred had introduced this treat and there was no going back. They had several months with Sheila insisting on sharing a room with her daughter before the wedding. While Fred never had any trouble communicating with women, his relationship with John continued to be a little more tricky in those early years. They often travelled in silence when Fred took John to school and later work. On a Sunday afternoon both Fred and John could be found in the back garden, cleaning and polishing their shoes for the week, again an activity conducted in silence most of the time, Fred being very particular about shoes being properly polished. No doubt Fred felt that John needed a strong male influence, while John had been the man of the house and despite his youth felt usurped. Nonetheless, Fred and John overcame the awkwardness of their early days, finding common ground over sport. In fact, as time went on, it became apparent that they shared a very similar sense of humour which bonded them, with John's impressions always collapsing Fred into laughter. Time was spent in the garden, which was carefully tended by Fred, who was a very keen gardener. He and Sheila would enter flowers and vegetables in the village fair every year. While John did not share the love of gardening, he and Fred would play cricket in the garden during the summer. John remembers Fred was a very decent spin bowler. This new family enjoyed a few holidays together in the early years. They all used to recall the first time Fred took them to his beloved Eastbourne. It seems they arrived at a Bed and Breakfast, ready to enjoy a few days together, but Fred was mortified to find there were nylon sheets on the bed. He quickly gathered his family and they left with the somewhat irate landlady shouting at them as they left. They found another hotel nearby and enjoyed their holiday but the experience of the nylon sheets was one which they recalled and laughed about frequently. Fred also took the family to France, not mentioning that he had been there during the war. They went to Nice, with Fred encouraging John, in particular, to speak French. John recalls he and Fred looking out over the beach and John's reaction to the topless bathers which Fred found very amusing. There was also a holiday to Jersey, which was enjoyed by all. John and Judith reflect on these holidays with a great sense of happiness, there was clearly a lot of laughter and fun shared.

While John had experienced some initial difficulties with Fred, Judith adored him from almost the first moment she met him. Being seven years older than John she instantly saw the connection between her mother and Fred, encouraging their romance. Fred in turn adored having a daughter and was particularly proud to walk her down the aisle on her wedding day in 1981. It was an experience he never thought he would enjoy and loved every minute of the day.

One decision early on which delighted Fred was Judith and John's decision to call him Dad. While he never attempted to usurp the memory of their own father, he took on the role of Dad with gusto. He never introduced Judith or John as his stepchildren, he always introduced them as his daughter or son, which was very touching and something that both Judith and John appreciated greatly. For John, in particular, his father had died when he was six, so his memories were few. Fred filled a void and due to their shared humour, unless told, people assumed Fred was his father.

I first met Fred in 1980, when going out with John, initially not knowing that Fred and Sheila had only been married for four years. They were a settled family and clearly at ease with each other and seemed like they had all been together forever. It was some time before I learned that they had only been a family for a short time. I feel that's a testament to Fred and Sheila who, having found happiness together, had been able to knit their family together seamlessly.

1980 was also the year that Fred was elevated to the board of the water company and became a director. Sheila was able to travel with Fred when he attended many conferences related to his work. They travelled to Japan and Brazil among other locations. They holidayed several times with Fred's lifelong friend Gordon Lyons and his wife. They had been at school together with Gordon performing as best man at both of Fred's weddings. This period to the end of the 1970s and first half of the 1980s were, for them, one long honeymoon.

Sheila had given up work, it was deemed inappropriate for her to continue to work at the water company with Fred as her boss. After seven years as a widowed single mother she enjoyed the freedom that marriage to Fred gave her. She provided a warm and happy home, which was always busy. Fred and Sheila hosted so many family parties, meetings for various clubs and societies, village groups; the house was a centre of entertaining. Frankly any excuse and there was a party, with Fred holding court, laughing and joking with all, making sure all had a glass of something while Sheila prepared wonderful food. Fred was infamous for his measures when pouring a drink with many referring to a Fred measure. Some friends will still often ask 'do you want a regular or Fred measure?'. It was particularly relevant for his favourite gin. My favourite photo of Fred is on his 60th Birthday, drink in hand as well as a cigar and laughing mightily with friends in his living room. They enjoyed a lively, active life, whether parties at home, dinners with friends, visits to the theatre and opera, all these events were enjoyed with gusto.

Sheila, after her marriage to Fred, could not simply sit back. She joined the Women's Institute, baking every Thursday for their Friday market in the village. The kitchen would be filled with wonderful aromas and the dining room would be stacked with food all packaged up and we were all under strict instructions not to touch anything, which was always infuriating. Flower arranging was a favoured hobby and she joined the local ladies in putting together wonderful arrangements for the local Catholic church. Beyond that she was willing to impart her wisdom, happily teaching those who were less experienced. With Fred a member of Rotary, Sheila joined Inner Wheel, which was the side of Rotary for women at the time. She made many friends and served with diligence, being President once. She loved art and took many art classes; family and friends are lucky enough to have some of her art in their homes. She was, without doubt, an accomplished artist and did exhibit occasionally.

Fred's professional life had been a success, retiring as a Director, Company Secretary and Treasurer of the Portsmouth Water Company in 1988. He would, though, remain a director until 1999. In the years leading up to 1988, he worked creatively and diligently to ensure that the Portsmouth Water Company could not be bought out by foreign investors. The planned privatisation of 1989 alerted many including foreign investors who wanted a piece of British utilities. Fred, while saying he had no strong feelings on privatisation, along with the board and trustees of the pension scheme, used the 1945 Water Act to let the water company pension fund buy a controlling interest in the company, thereby saving it from foreign control. The local paper, the *Portsmouth Evening News*, described the action as financial wizardry. Fred was quoted as saying that while the initial threat came from Britain, including the Southern Water Authority, the company had already managed to see off an approach from a French company.[84] Fred attempted to warn other water companies of the danger, particularly relating to foreign ownership of a utility, but he said his words fell, at least initially, on deaf ears. He was annoyed that by the time several of these companies realised what was happening it was too late for them to do anything and their independence and local connections were lost. While, publicly stating he had no strong feelings on privatisation, in private, he felt strongly that the water companies needed to keep a controlling interest. He foresaw the issues around big business having a financial interest serving shareholders rather than local companies focused on providing a service. The foresight of the management in the 1970s followed by Fred's creativity saved the Portsmouth Water Company and even today, decades after he left the business, it remains a local company focused on local needs. In 1990 the company listed on the stock exchange, but the prudence previously shown ensured that its focus would remain on providing a good service to its customers.[85] Fred had worked throughout this period with his good friend George Slater, who was the chief engineer and had joined the board at the same time as Fred. Despite their good friendship, they kept a close eye on each other's actions and the company's history describes their creative tension. Neither was afraid to call the other out if they felt intervention was required. This relationship powered the company forward during their tenure but never impacted their personal friendship. They would both, most days, head to the local pub on the corner for a pint at lunchtime. Other managers would join them and while this practice would be frowned on today, it was a time for camaraderie but also business. It certainly didn't impede the success of the company. If you popped in to see Fred in the late afternoon, his nose would normally

---

84 *Portsmouth Evening News*, date unknown. Personal papers of Fred Bailey

85 Andy Neve and Mike Hedges, *Portsmouth Water, 1857-2007*, Havant: Portsmouth Water Company, 2007, p.177

be in the pages of the *Financial Times*. He would, in later years, blame reading those pink pages leading to his requirement for reading glasses, although his eyesight was excellent generally.

Beyond that, Fred was a proud Rotarian, having joined the Portsmouth and Southsea club in 1975.[86] It was a part of his life that he enjoyed enormously, after his marriage to Sheila she had enthusiastically joined in and he used to take both John and Judith to the Sons and Daughters day which was held annually. He was a man who firmly believed in civic duty. When he served as President of the Portsmouth and Southsea club in 1981-1982, he was quite firm that the focus for his year was on enthusiasm. While he said the years of 1978-1980 had been hectic, he felt the previous year had been about fun and friendship, despite achievements. He said 'it was time for the club to take a deep breath and plunge back into Rotary activity with renewed vigour'.[87] He joined his good friend John Lindsey at the Rotary Housing Project in Portsmouth. This had been spearheaded by his friend and Fred found himself, along with colleagues from the water company, getting increasingly involved. The association provided, indeed continues to provide, sheltered housing for those in need in Portsmouth. Fred served as both vice chair and chairman of the Tenants Selection Committee and is credited as a great support to John Lindsey during his long tenure. Fred was, in 2006, awarded the Paul Harris Fellowship by Rotary, this was the year the number of people who had been awarded the Fellowship hit one million. It is awarded to individuals who have made a substantial contribution to the Rotary Foundation. He sat on the Gas Consumers Council for a time while still working. He instigated offering water company customers the opportunity to support WaterAid, firmly believing that all deserved fresh clean water. He also ensured support was given to local organisations. One instance was the water company printing calendars produced by students at a local school for those with learning disabilities in 1988, just before he retired.[88]

When their daughter and her husband emigrated to Australia in 1989, while sad at their departure, it opened up a new world for Fred and Sheila and they enjoyed multiple visits, usually for several months each time. They made new friends and were able to share in Jude and Rob's life in Australia and appreciated the life they had built.

---

86 Pers. Comms. Christopher Halliwell, October 2024

87 *Portsmouth Evening News*, 1980 but date unknown, personal papers of Fred Bailey

88 Personal papers, Fred Bailey

Closer to home, John and myself would provide Fred and Sheila with two much-loved grandchildren. Fred would pull the children, when toddlers, up the garden in his log truck, Sheila would bake them cakes and treats. They were very much part of the childrens lives, with the children remembering one particular day, when they took them out for a day to Marwell Zoo. Their over-riding memory is of Grandpa, driving around a roundabout five times attempting to work out which way to go! The grandchildren were a source of joy for them and they saw them regularly as John and his family lived locally to Fred and Sheila. We know they got immense pleasure from seeing the children grow into accomplished adults. Sheila, in her final hours, thanked John and Maxine for her beautiful family, a precious memory they hold.

It was one evening during dinner that Fred suddenly said that he had bought an elephant. The grandchildrens eyes lit up in awe at this comment and they then heard something of his adventures in Burma. As ever he gave a sanitised version of events and made it sound like a proper boy's own adventure, excitement peppered with humour.

While Fred returned to France multiple times and always enjoyed his visits. He made only one visit to Pertuis with Sheila. He found he didn't recognise much, as he said that most of the shops had been deserted during the war. He was disappointed that he didn't find anyone to talk to about his time there, life had moved on, although had he contacted the Marie (Mayor) one knows he would have been welcomed, but in keeping with the man, he didn't want to make a fuss. Some years later someone from the town did visit Fred at home in Sussex, bringing gifts, he greatly appreciated the opportunity to meet and speak with a member of the community and hear about the town. He slipped into speaking French with ease and it was impressive to see him chatting away. The very week Fred died the town buried one of their last resisters; such a shame they never got to meet in peacetime and swap stories, they would have likely known each other and had a unique connection. Fred never returned to Burma or Malaya, the closest he got was when he and Sheila visited Singapore.

Immediately after Fred retired, he and Sheila along with George and Joan Slater, took on a major trip which saw them visit Bali, Australia, New Zealand and California. They enjoyed a fun time, Fred and George having worked together for years were great friends and Sheila and Joan had become friends when she married Fred. The only time there was a minor bump in the trip was when George was pulled over by the police in New Zealand for speeding. Fred found it all quite hilarious but Sheila was mortified and worried lest they be booted out of the country and told never to return, which of course only caused more laughter on the part of Fred and George.

Once Fred retired, with more time on his hands, he served on the Bosham Parish Council, including a spell as Chairman. He was heavily involved in a twinning project for the village which saw him visit Honfleur more than once. While officially never twinned, there was a period when several reciprocal and highly enjoyable visits took place. Twinning of towns and villages began after the Second World War as a reconciliation across the continent and it was something Fred believed in strongly. He and Sheila enjoyed an active retirement, whether at home or travelling, the social whirlwind continued for them both and they loved every minute. Fred continued to attend Rotary for many years and in the latter years attended the Lucheoneers Club, consisting of fellow more mature Rotarians. Having joined the Rotary Club in Portsmouth while working, he remained an active member in retirement. The early decades meant a lunch out of the office and a few drinks, and a late return to the office. The style of working today means that lunchtime meetings are almost non-existent, but it was a different yet still productive time. He continued to be involved with the Rotary Housing Association in Portsmouth, attending meetings in Portsmouth and hosting meetings and events at home. Fred did though find time for other more relaxed pastimes, including golf which he played weekly until his mobility failed. He would usually play with a group of friends and John would join them when he could. Additionally, John and Fred would sometimes just play a round when work commitments allowed John to grab a day off. As Fred got older he dropped from playing 18 holes to 9 every week. When Sheila's health began to fail, it was an opportunity for Fred to get out of the house for a few hours and enjoy some company. He had already cared for one wife with ill health and it was clear that he felt desperately sad at Sheila's decline. She became dependent on oxygen and Fred cared for her during those final years. He would often refuse offers of help, preferring to be with her almost all the time. The weekly escape to golf gave him the respite he needed, so that he could return and care. He didn't cook though, they bought in ready meals and Fred would choose a good bottle of wine in the evening. His only foray into anything that might be considered cooking was his Welsh Rarebit, it might have been the only thing he could produce but it was fantastic and a real treat if he made it for you.

Fred and Sheila enjoyed a very happy marriage for over 30 years, with Sheila sadly passing away in 2013. Sheila, who had been widowed at a young age with two children, found in Fred a man who adored her and she adored him. She travelled globally with him, seeing places she had never imagined. She was inspired by Fred and their marriage had allowed her to support worthy causes.

The years following Sheila's death were inevitably difficult for Fred, but he never showed any great emotion. He enjoyed the company of family and friends and threw himself back into a social life that had been restricted by Sheila's failing health. He would give occasional talks to the Rotary Club, Catenians and even the village primary school, telling them a fairly standard tale of his time in the war.

With one of his best friends from Rotary, John Lindsey, he embarked on a holiday to Marseille - bear in mind he was over 90 at this point. They managed to travel down by train without mishap and enjoyed a week of good weather, good food and most importantly good wine. Having been given a mobile phone by the family, just in case he needed to contact us, he never switched it on. This caused his daughter some stress as she worried about him from Australia. Fair to say myself and John didn't worry at all, knowing that he and his great friend would be tripping the light fantastic and enjoying the wine. He laughed quite a lot on his return home, when told that Judith had been worried. He always said he didn't do stress, what was the point and felt this was a perfect example of unnecessary stress.

At the age of 92, Fred was awarded the Legion d'honneur by France, a second award for his service in the liberation of the country. The ceremony took place at the D-Day museum in Portsmouth, on 6 January 2016. While Fred had not participated in D-Day it was felt the most appropriate location. Captain Francois Jean, who was the honorary consul for France performed the ceremony with family and friends in attendance. It was a splendid event, and Fred was very proud to receive this additional recognition from the French, particularly as he had missed his ceremony for the Croix de Guerre, as he had still been fighting in the Far East at the time. He was interviewed by local television and gave his standard account of his war. It was fortunate that Judith and her husband were visiting for Christmas that year and were able to attend this special event. I spoke at the event, highlighting that even at that point very few were familiar with the incredibly brave and daring behaviour of people like Fred.

In 2017 Judith and her husband took the decision to temporarily move back to England. Fred had suffered some health issues in the years following Sheila's death and Judith, a trained nurse, felt that rather than hopping on a plane every time something happened it would be better to be here. Fred was at this time 92 when they returned. They anticipated having some holidays with him and being there to help him if he needed it for maybe a couple of years if they were lucky. They had only been back in the country for about six days when Fred fell ill. His heart which had given so much trouble when he was a small child decided it was time to be problematic again. He had suffered problems for some years, having stenosis, which is a hardening of the arteries. On this occasion it turned out to be a failing valve and unfortunately due to his heart's somewhat fragile state, he found himself moved to several hospitals over a period of six weeks before he was operated on. Despite the frail nature of his heart and the length of time he was in hospital, the operation was deemed a reasonable success, although he was warned that even the new valve was leaking a bit and that it would give him between three to five years. The only issue was that such an extended stay in hospital had impacted Fred's mobility substantially.

While Fred still managed some trips, a holiday to Norfolk as well as a few Special Forces Club events, increasingly his limited mobility led to him becoming more housebound. For a few years he still managed to get to the Lucheoneers Club on a Friday, but even these became less frequent.

Nonetheless, Fred still enjoyed socialising, with friends and family being constant visitors. Following Sheila's death, John and myself had instigated a Saturday night movie night at his house. He loved a pizza, the tiniest bit of salad - if it was green it really had no place on Fred's plate - along with a few unhealthy chips, which were very welcome. The movie always had to be an action one, the louder, the bloodier the better, his granddaughter did not always attend as she found his movie choice a bit rich for her. With the arrival of Judith and her husband they took over this tradition and we regularly still attended. The movie choice remained the same, comedies were out, we tried one once and that fell about as flat as a pancake. Fred's deafness meant that we could all happily have sat in another room and not missed a word but we all sat in the living room, eating pizza. Fred loved action movies, he would laugh till the tears came at anything violent or the incredulous stunts.

Some filmmakers have come across the SOE and the Jedburghs in more recent years with films such as *Allied* and very recently *The Ministry of Ungentlemanly Warfare*. Some are quite scathing of this type of entertainment, feeling the inaccuracies do a disservice. It's important to remember in these instances that the truth inspires and that artistic licence is inevitable. Fred certainly saw *Allied* and would have loved *The Ministry of Ungentlemanly Warfare,* and as was usual, he would have laughed uproariously through the action sequences.[89] He would be disappointed if those involved in the 'true' events were not acknowledged in some way but he also appreciated films for their entertainment value and realised that you simply couldn't always replicate the absolute truth for many reasons.

In the final years of Fred's life Mitch Utterback, a retired US Army Special Forces Lieutenant Colonel, made contact with Fred. He was in regular contact with Jack Singlaub and it gave Fred a great additional contact. As well as staying in contact and enabling through himself a contact with Singlaub, Utterback sent Fred some Jed wings, both in leather and metal, which Fred was delighted to receive. He also sent Fred a print by Samuel McIntire titled *'The Glorious Amateurs'*.[90] When it arrived from America, Fred looking at the radio operator depicted asked if it was him. He said it could have been as the image was a familiar one, likely it would have been familiar to all the Jeds. It hung proudly in his home until his death and now hangs in my office, a daily reminder of this brave group of men.

---

89 Guy Ritchie, *The Ministry of Ungentlemanly Warfare*
90 *The Glorious Amateurs* by Samuel McIntyre, Prairie Fire Art

CHAPTER SIX

SPECIAL FORCES CLUB AND EVENTS

The Special Forces Club was founded in London by Gubbins, who by this point was Major General in 1945, as he recognised that those who worked in the shadows could not share their experiences or discuss their war years with anyone. Every Jed was made a member when it opened, as well as members of SOE and other Special Forces. The club gave a safe haven, not to necessarily relive those difficult days but where there would be an understanding, a supportive network and a good bar. Over the years it was a sanctuary for many and a good spot to meet friends old and new. There was a safety in knowing you were among colleagues who understood something of your experiences. John Sharpe referred to it as quite posh, but said he never felt out of place there. While the Official Secrets Act stopped them from speaking openly, they all found in the club a sanctuary where they could reminisce. It was though primarily a social club and Fred enjoyed socialising. He had been one of the founding members and supported the club throughout his life, attending regularly, even in later years attending the many wonderful events the club hosted.

After his marriage to Sheila, he began taking her to the various events. One of the many wonderful events to be enjoyed enormously by Fred was the 70th anniversary of the founding of SOE, an evening held at the Imperial War Museum, at which looking at photographs was much enjoyed. After Sheila's death he looked to family and friends to accompany him to these special events. He took good friends to a club event at the Natural History Museum, in 2015 - which was used by SOE during the war. There had been a film in 1948, *Against the Wind*, which depicted a secret spy workshop hidden in the Natural

History Museum.[91] The film and its director, Charles Crichton, were slated, with at least one critic scoffing at the idea of a spy workshop in a place that housed dinosaurs. But when files were finally released in the 1990s, Crichton would have the last laugh; his film was eerily close to the truth. One of the writers of the film was J Elder Wills, who during the war was a Lieutenant Colonel, a film director recruited by SOE to head up their camouflage section – which just so happened to use the Natural History Museum. There was even an exhibition for spies to visit to see items that may have been of use to them. This really was a case of art imitating life. This film was overshadowed by the multiple successes of Crichton from *The Lavender Hill Mob* to *A Fish Called Wanda*, but perhaps his greatest achievement was in slipping *Against the Wind* past everyone. Whether Fred ever saw this film is unknown, but he and his friends thoroughly enjoyed their black tie evening at the museum celebrating its role in the secret side of the war. Fred met up with friends he had not seen for some time including a few American Jedburghs.

Another great club success was an evening at the Tower of London. On this occasion Fred took his son John, with both of them returning slightly the worse for wear on the train. Fred, laughing with his wonderful belly laugh, that told all he had enjoyed a good evening. At many of these events the Princess Royal was in attendance, as patron of the club and her support of the club was and is greatly appreciated. Fred loved the Princess Royal, he simply thought her wonderful and the letter the family received following Fred's death is testament to the impact he made on someone who meets so many during a very busy working life. At the Tower of London he had ensured that he was in the line to meet the Princess, moving around the room with John until he felt he was well positioned. John said he was like a schoolboy, trying to find the best spot to bump into the class favourite.

A particularly special weekend was organised by the Special Forces Club to coincide with Remembrance weekend in 2015. There was a service at St Margaret's Church in London. This church sits in the shadow of Westminster Abbey and is often called the parish church of the House of Commons. Fred gave a reading at the service before viewing the mounting number of crosses being placed around the Abbey. Following this there was a reception at St Ermin's Hotel, renowned for its links to the SOE and the secret services in general. This was a great evening, with Fred holding court and meeting and

---

91 IMDB, *Against the Wind*, Dir. Charles Crichton, 1948

talking with as many people as possible. He relied on son John to keep the food and wine flowing and John ensured the waiting staff passed by Fred with a regularity that ensured his glass was never empty. Other guests flocked to sit with him and just have a few words with one of the few remaining Jedburghs. John and myself barely spoke to Fred that evening, such was his popularity, only when the event finished did we retire to the bar for a final nightcap and chat.

That weekend, just short of his 92nd birthday, Fred took part in his first-ever march past the Cenotaph on Remembrance Sunday. It was the first time that the Special Forces Club had been allowed to participate. Although in a wheelchair, Fred ensured a tight formation and thoroughly enjoyed the experience. Fred would attend for three years and took those three visits to Remembrance Sunday in London very seriously; it was for the Jedburghs who had been killed that he proudly carried the wreath. He agreed to attend as it was the first opportunity that had been afforded to him but he was also there for all those comrades who were never allowed the opportunity. However, he was not there as a Jedburgh or member of SOE, but as a member of The Special Forces Club. He was a little disappointed to find that first year that they were lumped at the back just in front of the entertainers. He didn't deny anyone their place, but felt it was time the SOE and those who, both in Europe and the Far East, did so much, in such difficult circumstances, to aid the Allied victory to gain a bit of recognition from the British Establishment. They had received such positive receptions both in France and the United States, yet for the British Jedburghs, they were outside the lines. Sadly the issue with SOE was that it was not a regiment, sitting outside the military machine. The Jedburghs were soldiers but they had left their regiments behind. When honoured, such as the mention in despatches, it was always under their original regiment, which for Fred was the Royal Armoured Corps. For the wider SOE, most of their agents had never been in the military so they had no chance of marching past the Cenotaph. The freezing November weather meant that he felt after three visits he could not face another. It wasn't just the cold; he looked around at all those who had comrades to march with, all his friends were gone. As proud as he was to take part, he was immeasurably sad that he was the only Jedburgh, while John Sharp was still alive he chose not to attend. One amusing aside is that he always hoped to be interviewed by Sophie Raworth, of the BBC, who wanders among the veterans hearing their stories each year. His eye for the ladies was still strong in his 90s and while disappointed that the Jeds didn't get a wider airing on Remembrance Day, he felt he had done his bit quietly for them. Normally on Remembrance Day he would watch events on television at home, no doubt reflecting on those who had been lost during the war and the friends no longer around.

He took both Judith and Rob as well as John and myself to an evening event at Trinity House in 2017. This, like all the events, was a fabulous evening enjoyed by all. Fred did not have to manoeuvre himself into position to meet the Princess Royal on this occasion, he was, along with other veterans, lined up to meet her. The last club event he was able to attend was at St Paul's in London, a year later, again a wonderful evening in a wonderful setting with great company. When during a conversation with the family, he realised that he had never taken his son or daughter or their partners to the actual Special Forces Club, he said he wanted to go one last time. Unfortunately, by this time Fred's health was declining with very limited mobility and the decision was taken that the journey, involving many hours in a car, would be too exhausting and he reluctantly accepted that he would not be able to enjoy a final gin and bitter lemon in the club which had meant so much to him.

However, it was more than just a jolly social club. Resistance leaders from across Europe met there, indeed they were members. The significant network that Gubbins had built at SOE did in some ways simply transfer to the club. Those who had not known each other during the war met and became friends, influence continued. In the authorised biography of Gubbins by Brian Lett, he quotes Gubbins in 1964, stating - and this is paraphrased - that many of those who had been involved with SOE were either in high positions in governments across Europe or at least were influencers. He cites the Danish equivalent club as being instrumental in bringing Denmark into NATO. He said the club had two objectives: somewhere for those who had served to meet and have somewhere to stay, but the second objective was about maintaining, strengthening and furthering the goodwill across Europe and Asia that they had fostered. He wanted mutual understanding and to create a happier world. A noble man indeed and one that Fred had the highest regard for.

JEDBURGH REUNIONS

One of things Fred always said he was impressed and proud of was how the Jeds kept in touch. They had a bond that ensured they stayed in contact, with the British Jeds having reunions every four years. The Americans did likewise but it wasn't until the 1980s that the veil of secrecy lifted and they could enjoy more public reunions. There was, of course, sadness that many were missing from these reunions. For Fred, the French member of Team Citroen, Pierre Bloch was killed in the Algerian War when he stepped on a mine. His and other losses such as

Gardner stayed with Fred. Sheila said that she sat and listened to what was being said at these reunions during the 1980s and wondered what on earth they were talking about. She asked Fred and he told her a very limited amount; he believed he had endured so that others did not need to hear the full story of his experiences. Over the years and reunions she learned more but Fred was very humble and never discussed it more widely for many years. Additionally for these men, having not been able to talk about their war for decades meant they found it quite difficult to suddenly talk to all and sundry about events they had been told they could never speak of. However, Fred thoroughly enjoyed the reunions and they were opportunities to meet old friends who had a shared experience, and he always attended if he could. Reunions took place both in Britain, France and the United States and were the one place he could relax and talk to others who understood.

The first formal reunion in 1984 followed an invitation from the then Mayor of Paris, Jacques Chirac. There is a photograph of the Jeds spread out in the shape of a parachute at the Mont Valerian memorial which remains a striking memento. One Jedburgh, Jacques Martin of Team Chloroform, was at this time the deputy head of the Direction Politique in the French Foreign Ministry, and Mitterrand was President of France, who himself had been in the Resistance and had been flown out of Tangmere by Hugh Verity. This was an emotional reunion for the men, meeting old comrades, swapping stories of both the past and present. For them all to be back in France together was an extraordinary experience; a country they all loved and had fought to free had invited them back. It opened a door which had been closed for many and allowed a breath of air to sweep through and for, at least a moment, they were not in the shadows but able to stand tall and tell something of their stories. This reunion made the national news in the UK and beyond. Very slowly and quietly stories emerged, books written yet this small band of men remain to this day still shrouded in secrecy, unless you know where to look. Even then the full story is never and will never be told.

A very moving reunion for Fred was held in the United States in 1988, almost one hundred of the original three hundred were able to reunite. A ceremony at Arlington National Cemetery, where the names of the dead were read out by a former Jed of the relevant nationality was particularly moving. Fred joked that the Green Berets had given them a demonstration of modern tactics and they all agreed that they wouldn't be able to do any of it anymore. Fred said it all looked a bit hair-raising, but likely the Green Berets would have thought what Fred and the other Jedburghs did was hair-raising. Beyond that there was a visit to the White House with President Reagan making an appearance and sending a special message. This group of slightly greying men with their impressive medals worn proudly were able to stand tall during this visit, they were acknowledged and treated with both kindness and respect. It was a visit enjoyed by all.

Other reunions followed, both formal and informal. Reunions in England followed with a reunion at Milton Hall in 1991, which was particularly special for all. Memories flooded back with reflections on their training and the place where the Jeds were born. Fred always reflected on his time at Milton Hall as a good time in his life. He would say it had been hard work, but the camaraderie of that time was a very special memory. What is very clear from the photos of reunions was the sheer joy that Fred felt at these occasions; you can see the smile in his eyes, which always spoke, telling of his pleasure at these occasions.

They were also very well received in France and in 1994 on the 50th anniversary of the liberation, a reunion in Normandy, as guests of the Americans, was much enjoyed. It's both interesting and telling that they were guests of the Americans, the British apparently not involving them. Fred was certainly a man who enjoyed a good event and good glass of wine, as did many of the Jeds, so these events were usually filled with laughter and stories.

There was another reunion at Milton Hall, with a service at Peterborough Cathedral, in 1996 when a memorial plaque was unveiled at the Cathedral, commemorating the thirty-seven Jedburghs who lost their lives, either in Europe or the Far East.

While he attended many reunions with Sheila, he was more guarded with the wider family. We didn't always know about the reunions until after they had occurred. There were likely a few reasons for this; he always assumed no one was interested, despite our repeatedly stating our interest. Also these events related to a past life and he both wanted to retain them for himself, an opportunity to revisit a past that the family were not part of, which seems quite understandable. In 2001 John and I did, however, attend a reunion at Tangmere Military Aviation Museum, a marquee pitched in front of the museum and a good mix of both Jedburghs and families attended. Having been the archivist there I know there is a printed version of the poem Tangmere Lizzie by Douglas Littlejohn, which is signed by several Jeds and family members in the archives. This reunion, over a weekend, had included a reception at Arundel Castle in their honour as well as a visit to the D-Day Museum in Portsmouth, and there was also a lunch at Amberley, near Arundel. This particular weekend saw forty-three

Jedburghs attend with two from America. They had, by this point, increased reunions to every two years rather than the previous four years. This was, in part, due to diminishing numbers, they were all getting older and they knew there would come a point when they would not be able to get together anymore. It was at this reunion that Jack Singlaub gave Fred a copy of his book, with a personal inscription, which now sits on my bookshelf. There was also a reunion at the *Cutty Sark*, to which apparently sons and daughters were invited; we know Judith and her husband would have been in Australia and it's possible that it occurred at a time when we were not living locally. These Jedburgh reunions were clearly very special to Fred and all who attended, the years could slip away and they could recall shared experiences whether it was during training or in the field.

Many Jeds kept some memorabilia of their war experiences, but Fred did not actively keep mementos. He thought he had kept his silk map, but the only item we have found was the card, in English and French, advising that he was in France to aid its liberation. Harrington Museum is worth a visit as it holds the memorabilia of several Jedburghs including Verlander and Trofimov.

There were, sadly, a number of Jedburghs who survived their European operations, but were killed in the Far East, whether they were British, French or American. Nevertheless, for those who survived, it's worth taking a moment to look at the post-war lives of some of the Jeds. Fred was a sergeant in the British Army, not an officer despite being recommended for a commission, but like so many Jeds he went on to enjoy a career which put him at the top of his profession. One can only assume that the testing that these men went through to get into the Jeds was able to identify some traits that no doubt signified not just success in the theatre of war but also in life generally.

They were, as a group, pretty extraordinary. Militarily, Aaron Bank of Team Packard would go on to form the 'Green Berets' America's Special Forces, having lobbied for a Special Forces unit. He based the training and structure on his own experiences with the Jedburghs in France and the Far East. Even the original name of 10th Special Forces Group was deliberately unconventional, suggesting there were another nine groups somewhere. Today the US Special Forces can look to the Jedburghs as the inspiration for their existence. After his military career he was significant in ensuring US nuclear power facilities improved their security, being tenacious in tackling this subject. Jack Singlaub of Team James went on to have a prominent career. Like so many Jeds, he headed east after France and with a team parachuted into the Red River Delta to blow bridges on strategic routes.[92] He was appointed as the CIA deputy station chief in Seoul, but couldn't leave his adventurous escapades behind. He developed and carried out high-altitude parachute drops over the Han River. He understood the potential advantages of parachuting agents from high altitude while also incorporating low level parachute opening. This idea no doubt inspired by his Jedburgh experiences. His career continued and in true Jedburgh spirit at the rank of Brigadier General and at the age of 51 he attended flight school as he realised the importance of helicopters in special operations. In 1977 he publicly questioned President Carter's plans in the Korean Peninsula and was relieved of his duty for failing to respect the President's position as Commander-in-Chief. Less than a year later he again questioned the President's national security policies and was forced to retire.[93] In 2015 the US Special Forces Command created the John Singlaub award, in honour of his achievements both on and off the battlefield. It is presented annually to a member of the US Special Forces.

When a couple of years after the war, the Americans realised the relevance of an intelligence service. They had closed OSS down, as the British had shut SOE, but Britain had its SIS and MI departments, where America had none. Wild Bill Donovan, who had worked so well at the OSS would be denied a role in the new organisation, yet he contributed from the sidelines for a few years before his untimely death from dementia.

William Colby of Team Bruce would become the head of the CIA during a particularly difficult time for the agency and some say that he saved it from itself in the wake of investigations. He had joined the CIA when it was created and spent around 12 years in the field in various parts of the world including the Far East.[94] Like Singlaub, he would also write a book about his life. The leader of Team Frederick, British Major Adrian Wise, stayed in the army for his career, retiring as a Brigadier in the early 1970s. A number of French Jedburghs, including Jean Sassi, were instrumental in the setting up the French Special Forces in the post-war years.

Beyond the military, the Jedburghs produced a British Member of Parliament, Neil Marten of Team Veganin. George Millar wrote many books including several on his time during the war. Bernard Knox went on to a distinguished academic career. Born in Britain, he

---

92 Singlaub, *Hazardous Duty*, p. 79
93 Ibid
94 Irwin, *The Jedburghs*, p.229

graduated from Cambridge. After the war he emigrated to the United States, completing his master's degree at Harvard and his PhD at Yale, for more than 20 years he was the Director of Hellenic Studies at Harvard.[95] Several American Jedburghs would go on to work for the CIA. Many of the American Jedburghs were able to continue their education under the GI bill with several lawyers among them. Many like Fred simply returned to their pre-war lives and got on with living.

Harry Verlander, a fellow radio operator, would join the railway and hold a role with British Continental Services, specifically with the car ferry side of the business, where his fluent French was put to good use. Harry would return to France and marry his French sweetheart, whom he met while with Team Harold. The marriage ultimately failed, but he went on to two further marriages and his widow, Elizabeth, continues to promote and support the memory of the Jedburghs.

John Sharpe worked for British Steel and lived a full life in Surrey. John and Fred kept in touch by phone when meeting became too arduous for them both. John's death in 2019 was a blow for Fred; his last British Jed friend was gone.

For Colin Gubbins, with the closing of SOE in 1946, he found himself retired out of the army. His unconventional ways were not fully appreciated. Churchill, who had been a supporter, was out of office and the excuse seems to have been that there were too many senior officers. He was given the honorary rank of Major General; it was certainly honorary as his pension was that of a colonel. The New Year's Honors list delivered him a knighthood. But the British establishment missed a trick, here was a man whose knowledge and connections across Europe were second to none and who in the post-war years could have been invaluable to the country. He was 49 years old and unemployed, he did find employment, he was simply too good not to and found a job in a textile and carpet company, learning the trade and becoming Managing Director. It had eleven factories across England and it was noted that he could walk into any one of them and know every employee. His remarkable skills were not wasted but the British establishment lost out due really to politics. He was not always popular for being unconventional with the army, and poilticians didn't always like his interventions, whether diplomatically or directly political. There's no doubt though that his connections were extraordinary.

Irwin, in his book *The Jedburghs*, makes the salient point that you could walk into a room full of Jedburghs and they could discourse on multiple subjects from the classics to epidemiology, law or opera

---

95 Irwin, The Jedburghs

but they could also knock you on your ass.⁹⁶ This description is, in a nutshell, the Jedburghs.

FRED AND INTERVIEWS
With the dwindling numbers of Jeds left, Fred found himself increasingly popular, be it for print interviews or television. He had mixed emotions about this attention, on one hand there is no doubt he enjoyed the attention. But he spoke out of sense of duty, for those who were no longer around. He was often asked if he had been scared during his service, his response was blunt, 'if you were scared, you were dead'.⁹⁷

He was always surprised that anyone was interested in what he had done all those years ago, he thought younger people would be bored to hear an old man talking about the war. Yet younger people were fascinated by this aspect of the war; personal stories and secret operations are a potent mix and make the reality of war a little more tangible.

Fred had been interviewed by the Imperial War Museum and his oral history is openly available. Martyn Cox of Legasee recorded another interview with Fred, as well as multiple other veterans, which is available online.⁹⁸ Martyn Cox arranged in 2016 for Fred to be interviewed on Radio 4.⁹⁹ He thoroughly enjoyed this experience and in Martyn Cox found someone genuinely intrigued and fascinated by the stories of Fred and others who had fought in the shadows. Martyn Cox remains an advocate for the Special Operations Executive and all who served within it, he co-founded the Secret WW2 Learning Network Charity.

In 2018 Fred was approached about a tv programme about the RAF at 100 years old.¹⁰⁰ The director, Harvey Lilley and one of the producers Josh Grant came to visit Fred at home. They chatted for a while and were genuinely interested in Fred's story, particularly around his escape in a Lysander from Burma. They were about to leave when the story of buying the elephant was told and they promptly sat down again and stayed a little longer. Ultimately Fred was invited to take part in the programme, quite the honour as obviously he had served in the

---

96   Irwin, *The Jedburghs*, p. xxii
97   Pers. Comms
98   Legasee, https://www.legasee.org.uk/
99   *Spooks, Spies and Videotapes*, Robert Elms, Radio 4, 2015
100 Dir. Harvey Lilley, *RAF at 100*, BBC, 2018

army. But in reviewing the 100 years of the RAF the programme makers realised that the special operations during the Second World War had relied on the RAF, whether it was dropping supplies to the Resistance or taking agents in. Fred himself had been dropped by an American crew in a Liberator going into France. However, what intrigued the programme makers was his escape from Burma in the Lysander. It seems they attempted to locate the flight and find out who had flown the team to safety, years and documents lost in the midst of war meant that the closest they came was to determine that the pilot was likely Australian. Fred could not remember the pilot, only that they thanked him when they landed in safety. While family and friends had been impressed at the prospect of the programme and of Fred meeting Ewan and Colin McGregor, Fred was oblivious as to who Ewan McGregor was, asking if he had seen anything he had been in, films were reeled off to Fred as he shook his head. Nonetheless he found the brothers charming and genuinely interested, which if Fred sensed a genuine interest, he would happily engage. He thoroughly enjoyed the day filming, in June 2017, at the Shuttleworth Collection in Bedfordshire. He spent time deep in conversation with both Mary Ellis and Joy Lofthouse. These two incredible women who had flown with the ATA were wonderful characters who kept everyone amused and occasionally gasping at their tales. The evening before filming, Fred and I were in the bar, frankly where else would you find us, when Mary Ellis walked in, ramrod straight, no stick in sight. Fred who was using a walker by this time was determined to look good and insisted on my keeping the walker out of sight. He did his best but had to admit defeat and use the walker but only after walking out of the bar. He wanted to make a good impression with the ladies and a walker wasn't going to cut it in his mind. We enjoyed a wonderful evening with both Mary and Joy, who were both clearly seasoned when it came to interviews and tv appearances.

After this there was a series called *Secret Agent Selection*, a reality-type programme putting members of the public through an SOE style selection process.[101] Many were sceptical of the programme, worried that a reality programme would demean or diminish the important work of the SOE. Fred though felt that if it shone a light on those that served it would be worthwhile, and agreed at least to an initial meeting. He met with a producer and was interviewed and waited to hear if they needed him. The director was Emma Frank and when they came to film Fred at home, he found the crew genuinely interested.

---

101 Dir. Emma Frank, *Secret Agent Selection*, BBC, 2018

With the crew that day Fred met Robert Copsey, one of the finalists. He was an ex-army man who had been injured in combat - while only two minutes made it onto the screen, the two men chatted for around five hours. Fred found in Rob a kindred spirit who understood war and what it meant to serve. Fred enjoyed the programme when it was aired declaring it a success, his only complaint being the way the contestants wore their berets. Fred recognised the need to employ different mediums to tell what is a difficult story.

Fred lived locally to the former RAF Tangmere, now a wonderful museum, and had enjoyed at least one Jedburgh reunion there. Despite the Jeds never having flown from there it has a strong link to the SOE, being a take-off point for many agents. Old friends were able to catch up over lunch in a marquee and while they often didn't speak of their war experiences there was a camaraderie between these men and the bond between them was obvious to observers. Fred was also delighted to be invited along when the museum acquired a replica Lysander. It had been used in the film, *Allied*, starring Brad Pitt.[102] It was Pitt it seems who insisted that the Lysander be built as an accurate replica. The museum was able to secure it with some initial advice from Martyn Cox and it now forms a wonderful display telling some of the story of the SOE. RAF Tangmere was the station used by the Lysanders. Close to the coast, it was ideally placed for the Lysanders to hop across the channel and drop off agents and bring them and others back.

As well as the unveiling of the Lysander, Fred was invited along again, in August 2018, when several of the contestants of *Secret Agent Selection* went to the museum. This was a great day, comprising talks and displays with Fred being feted by all there. It was a day he thoroughly enjoyed, looking at items brought along for the day as well as enjoying the museum and talking to many people, most of whom wanted their photo taken with him. He was happy to oblige and absolutely loved it.

Fred wanted to hit 100, but his body decided that 99 was far enough, as he would have said he made his 100th year, not bad for someone born with a heart condition. He died peacefully, a fate many who served did not enjoy.

It can be difficult to separate the man who fought in the war and the gentle quiet soul, who many may have viewed as a regular accountancy type of company man. The thing is he was both of these men. None of us are the people we were when we were young, so it stands to reason that Fred would be different as well.

---

102 Dir. Robert Zemeckis, *Allied*, 2016

CHAPTER SEVEN

REFLECTIONS

The noted SOE historian M R D Foot quoted Gubbins as saying that 'The Jedburghs had been absolutely wasted by not being pushed in at once'.[103] While it speaks to the frustration felt by many Jeds including Fred, it would be wrong to simply focus on this fact. Instead it should be appreciated that this was an amazing and unique unit. Not only that, they achieved incredible results overall, while being failed at almost every point by those in command in the field.

They were a multi-national force, which alone was extraordinary at the time, and should really be celebrated for the success it was. The Jedburghs were a success, even official documents state that and every one of these men, although no longer with us, should be celebrated for being part of such a groundbreaking innovation.

The fact they all got on so well that decades later they could meet up and pick up where they left off is frankly amazing. It was one of the things that Fred was most impressed by and proud of. It is necessary to remember that this was the 1940s, people didn't go overseas for holidays, America was a far-off country that people only knew through the movies. France was equally unknown, yet men from these three nations came together under a common banner to fight for their own and our freedom.

Fred always said he didn't reminiscence. While he talked to Sheila in the early days about his first wife, she was never mentioned more generally. When Sheila died he simply repeated *I don't do reminiscence* and she was rarely mentioned. A photo of her though remained constantly in his eyeline when he was sitting in his armchair. This wasn't because he hadn't cared, it was simply his coping mechanism, always in the moment. This was why Fred had initially shied away

---

103 Lett, *SOE's Mastermind*, p.229

from speaking much about his war experiences, as said earlier. Only when numbers reduced did Fred accept the need to pick up the Jed baton and carry it that last mile; he didn't want the Jedburghs to simply be a footnote in history.

In his later years, he gained some pleasure from reflecting on his role in the war; he felt he had contributed and done his bit. The interviews and the award of the Legion d'Honneur all confirmed to him that he had made a worthwhile contribution. I think there was some regret that the Jeds perhaps never received a level of recognition he felt they deserved in Britain - the price of secrecy ran long. The decades of secrecy had made him assume no-one would be interested, he often found it almost amusing when someone wanted to talk to him. He would sometimes watch interviews of old soldiers recalling their experiences and say quietly, 'they haven't a clue', this was never meant to demean anyone's experiences at all, but Fred knew so many who had done so much, who never spoke of their actions. The secret nature of the Jeds meant that they had to look on as others were lauded, but they took quiet satisfaction in knowing their truth.

While everyone loves secrets, it's not always possible to delve into the secrets of the past. But we can tell something of a few of these brave men, the men on the ground, behind enemy lines, their everyday lives interrupted before those that survived were reabsorbed into anonymity in civvy street.

Fortunately there are many who have realised the importance of the Jedburghs and the clandestine work done and who work to ensure the deeds of the men are remembered and honoured.

There remain mysteries of course, famously the photo of Fred with what appears to be a German badge on his beret. In an unguarded moment when asked, he flippantly responded 'Oh I took that off an SS officer I shot' - almost immediately he pleaded ignorance, saying he couldn't remember where he got it. The truth will never be known; quiet moments with comrades may have allowed the barriers to drop, but never publicly.

We have seen that the Jedburghs in France worked, in many cases, far too briefly but with enormous energy and bravery to ensure the Resistance was as ready and able as possible. They slowed the German advance and their retreat, preventing reinforcements and generally caused a nuisance. Eisenhower acknowledged the work of the Resistance and the SOE in a letter to Gubbins, in May 1945.[104] They also

---

104 Foot, *SOE in France*, p.441

provided vital information on enemy locations and movements which aided the advancing troops. There were, without doubt, shortcomings, but they were not the fault of the Jeds. These men were so much more than just a group of soldiers, they were highly trained commandos. Beyond that they had the skills and ability to train, lead, advise and very importantly negotiate. Whether they fought or negotiated with either Germans for their surrender or dealt with the Maquis groups who at times were more interested in fighting each other, these men left a legacy for others if they know where to look.

Fred's time in Burma was difficult to put it mildly, not just the enemy but the jungle itself proved to be an adversary. Looking back to those 4 hours of first-aid training, Fred's reputation as a doctor can be seen as somewhat humorous, but it goes to the soldier-diplomat role. He aided the locals and built respect and trust, the situation was dire as time went on but these men never forgot their training or their duty.

They are a section of SOE that draws debate, sent in too late, sidelined - all these comments have merit. But behind this were well trained men, willing and able to do whatever was asked of them. Often let down, with limited supply runs, poor drops causing, at best damaged equipment and at worst lost lives, and a lack of understanding of their role by many, including the hierarchy of the regular army. Yet in spite of these issues, this was said to be one of the most decorated units of the war. The British radio operators who went into the field were almost to a man mentioned in despatches, beyond this a few received the Military Medal. This is extraordinary for a small 'reserve' force. They were also awarded honours by France; at least thirty of the British radio operators being awarded the Croix de Guerre.

The people of France and Burma had been living under occupation and suddenly here were men in Allied uniforms telling them it was time for action. The morale boost alone would have been substantial and should not be underestimated. It is worth remembering that this group consisted of both professional soldiers and those classed as unprofessional, like Fred, who simply joined up for the war. The fact that they all worked together in such a new and untried way with so many successes is surely the thing to focus on. Many teams crossed enemy lines to feed information back to the advancing troops. Whether it was Team Cedric who survived or Team Augustus who were all killed, this was real war, up close and very personal. For Fred, as a radio operator, he had some protection, left behind on some recces to protect the lines of communication. Nonetheless, there was continual jeopardy, Fred, as previously mentioned, would say they often had warnings of incoming German patrols, but there was a real risk of betrayal. It was not unknown for the Resistance to have German sympathisers, and SOE suffered many instances of betrayal which cost lives. It was often said of SOE that the radio operators had a life expectancy of six weeks, sadly for some it was less. Also, several of the men enjoyed relationships while in France, Fred certainly did, but it's worth bearing in mind that even this was fraught with danger. There was the constant risk of betrayal by those purporting to be friends, also the danger for any woman involved with an Allied soldier was extreme should the Germans, who were still active in most areas, find out. At this point in the war punishments were brutal towards the Resistance and anyone who aided or befriended them.

Another question which has to be asked is, what was the actual value of the Jeds and Resistance overall. Economics obviously enter the discussion. When it comes to the SOE including the Jeds, it is worth contemplating that Bomber Command's total losses in terms of dead was four times SOE's entire strength. The argument in economics is that subversive war is far more economical both in terms of people and it can be argued in terms of effectiveness. Hundreds of bombers with crews may look impressive, cause destruction and provide propaganda, but the quiet saboteur can cause disruption with a single targeted attack. Factories and rail lines were effectively targeted in France, causing minimal casualties to civilians but regular havoc for the German war machine. As stated in the Introduction irregular warfare has been shown through the ages to be effective, but it was a difficult concept for some in both political and military circles to comprehend and this, for the Jedburghs in particular, caused problems. The Resistance itself was also very effective in France, and in spite of the years under occupation, the Jedburghs found thousands willing and ready to rise up and reclaim their country. Issues post-war in terms of France's acknowledgement of assistance is more complex but we can take a simple view and recognise as previously noted that the country needed to rebuild and while accepting assistance it needed to feel it had accomplished much on its own. When you look collectively across France rather than focusing on individual teams you realise that the Jedburghs achieved an enormous amount. From providing an immediate morale boost, they trained and armed thousands, they brought leadership where it was needed and confidence where it may have been flagging. There are instances of tragedy, bravery, cooperation, diplomacy, and comradeship; all of these were offered and accepted by those they came into contact with.

As we have seen many of the Jedburghs went on to great things post-war and even those who may be called ordinary men, reached the pinnacle of their careers and enjoyed success through their lives. They have left a legacy with their children and grandchildren, many of whom work tirelessly to ensure their stories are not lost to time.

For a man born with a heart condition and who, in spite of that, did all that he did, it was a remarkable life. One comment following the publication of his obituary in the *Daily Telegraph* said, for someone with a heart condition, he could probably have sat out the war, instead he threw himself into dangers that were unimaginable. Fred was not someone who would have ever sat on the sidelines, he wanted to live his life, which meant doing something and like all the Jeds, it was not for the glory or the medals, it was because it was the right thing to do. This continued in his post war life, his sense of civic duty was unrelenting.

Fred was, it is believed, the last Jed left. While he had a certain pride in that, he was also quite sad. All his pals from those days were gone, there was no-one he could look in the eye and see an understanding of what they had each experienced. He had lost the women he loved and was left with his memories, which he did not always enjoy reflecting on.

While you may be reading this to learn about the Jedburghs and that is the vital role of this book, for us the family, we remember the humour and good nature of a quiet humble man.

As stated at the beginning, Fred was an ordinary man but on reflection one has to ask - were the Jeds just ordinary men? No has to be the answer, they were extraordinary men, every one of them. The rigorous selection process, the intense training and ultimate skills they developed tapped into something these men already possessed. Various terms could be used, loyal, intelligent, resourceful, quick-witted, as well as skilled commandos - the list could go on, these men had qualities that were picked up during selection and shows that there was a method to the assessments which stood the test of time. Every one of them was extraordinary.

Following Sheila's death, Fred gave out instructions to the family regarding his own death. He left strict instructions for his war medals; no-one was ever to wear them. He had earned them and they were not for others to glorify either him or his service. The family have kept them and they will, it is hoped pass down the generations.

Fred died on 29 January 2023. His health had been gradually failing but his decline accelerated in the final months. He was cared for at home by his daughter with a team of carers coming in to offer a little extra support. His health declined rapidly around Christmas 2022, and he passed away with his daughter by his side; we arrived just minutes after he passed away.

With Fred being the last Jedburgh, his funeral was well attended by Special Forces Club members and serving members of the Special Forces and the relatively new Ranger Regiment. The service was conducted in the village church where King Harold had prayed before setting sail for France in 1064. Fred would have enjoyed his funeral, and would have been particularly pleased to see everyone enjoying a drink on him afterwards. Fred had often contributed to or organised obituaries for other Jeds, so the pressure was on to ensure his was a good one. Thanks to the diligent work of Charles Owen with input from Stephen Kippax, Paul McCue and myself, Fred would have been very satisfied with it and the multitude of positive comments which followed its publication. In fact, he would have been surprised at the number of positive comments and the warmth directed towards him. His standard, 'didn't think anyone would be interested' comes to mind.

The Jedburghs deserve their place in British history, a wartime entity that suffered jealousy and infighting among establishment really ought to be brought in from the cold and acknowledged more widely.

Fred was a man with a great sense of humour, who said he never knew what stress was, what was the point. If nothing else we could all learn that lesson - don't stress.

APPENDIX

ACKNOWLEDGEMENTS

The decision to write this book was a family one and I have to thank my husband, John and children Zoe and Josh for their unwavering support. My sister in law, Judith and her husband Rob have not only supported this work but greatly assisted in finding photographs and reminding me of stories.

My thanks also to Stephen Kippax and Paul McCue, who reduced substantially the number of hours I spent at the National Archives by providing me with multiple files. Simon Leney, son of Jed Roger, kindly provided one photo, our family one wasn't as good! Additionally he kindly allowed me to read his father's memoir. Thanks must go to Martyn Cox, one of the founders of the Secret WW2 Learning Network which is such an excellent organisation. Martyn is also behind the Legasee project which has recorded so many veterans for posterity. Thanks are due to the multiple individuals who work to keep the Jedburgh history alive, including Clive Bassett, son of Jed Cyril, who works with Harrington Museum and runs the Jedburgh Facebook group.

My thanks also to Nigel Atkins, who employed me on another project, *Secret Operations over Occupied Europe*, without which this book would likely have not been written. Thanks also to Lisa Hooson, Stephen Chumbley and all at Pen and Sword for their support.

Of course this work would not have been possible without Fred and the other Jeds, it's so important that these men and their stories are not lost to history. My thanks to them for their service and for sharing at least some of their experiences.

OTHER TEAMS SENT INTO FRANCE FROM ALGIERS

TEAMS DESPATCHED FROM NORTH AFRICA

Beyond Team Citroën and those other teams despatched on the same night, a total of twenty-four teams were sent from Algeria. This would have been a tight group, who spent months living and training in North Africa and had become friends.

These teams and brief details of their missions are contained below.

AMMONIA
2 AMERICAN, 1 FRENCH, 9/10 JUNE

Dropped to the Wheelwright circuit, run by George Starr, their role was to equip and utilise guerrilla forces between Montauban and Bordeaux on rail, road and communication links. Reinforced with second radio operator during operation. The team found the Maquis in their area in great need of training and that there were too many people trying to give orders to various Maquis. They commented that they received excellent material.

BUGATTI
2 FRENCH, 1 AMERICAN, 28/29 JUNE
Major Fuller, Capt. De la Roche, S/Lt. Guillemot

Dropped to the Pyrenees area to work with the Wheelwright circuit, to assist in developing the area and engage in harassing the enemy on all lines of communication. They were also tasked with laying on reception for large-scale daylight troop drops. They liaised well with George Starr, who ran Wheelwright and agreed a location and set about multiple sabotage operations. They were attacked by a substantial number of German troops but they and the Maquis evaded without injury, managing to inflict some damage on the enemy. The team suffered betrayal with their position given to the enemy; they stated they had more to fear from the French than the Germans at times. Nonetheless they managed to stay one step ahead with diplomatic skills tested due to an ongoing lack of arms or explosives which made the team's position difficult as they were unable to deliver the promised arms. Once given the order to move against the enemy more fully, they were able to ensure that the Maquis were as effective as possible. Lack of supplies caused issues that could have been avoided and the Maquis could have done more had they been supported with arms and explosives, but there simply wasn't enough to go around.

CHLOROFORM
2 FRENCH, 1 AMERICAN, 29/30 JUNE
Capt. Martin, Lt McIntosh, Lt. Sassi

An unusual task of re-establishing resistance in the Drome Hautes Alps region which had been disorganised by 'heroic but ill-timed action' of Lt Alain against non-military targets. This was the third mission the team had been briefed for and when they arrived discovered that political misunderstandings was not the issue and that sabotage was going well in the area. The team moved to the Hautes Alpes area where they felt they could do more good. They implemented training for those on the ground and were able to mobilise the Maquis and assist the advancing Americans.

CHRYSLER
2 BRITISH, 1 FRENCH, 16 AUGUST
Capt. Sell, Lt. Aussaresses, Sgt. Chatten

Dropped to the Ariege area to liaise with the Detective circuit. Their first attempt at dropping was aborted by the pilot as no lights were seen at the drop zone. This delay led to a change in emphasis. When they did leave their drop was too fast and from too high meaning that the team and their containers landed in various locations up to 3 kilometres from the drop zone. The team had a busy time working with the Maquis. They had to intervene when they heard of executions and discussed with Maquis chiefs the suspension of executions pending instructions for court martials. This was a delicate time with teams having to attempt to contain the understandable desire for vengeance against the occupier.

TEAM CINNAMON
Previously discussed

TEAM CITROEN
Fred's Team, previously discussed

COLLODIAN
1 BRITISH, 1 FRENCH, 1 AMERICAN, 6/7 AUGUST
Capt. Hall, Lt. Marsaudon, Sgt Baumgold

Flown in to join Quinine and offer support following the death of Arete. They found little use for them in the original location although they worked with the Maquis to resolve friction between groups. They then moved to Entraygues to assist the Maquis, who were proving adept at sabotage yet sadly reprisals were brutal. The team reported a horrendous crime perpetrated by the Germans against civilian prisoners, made to dig their own graves, then shot in them before being savagely beaten. The team had some difficulty convincing local maquis on the best way to hold a town tactically, the team reported stormy scenes before their advice was taken.

DODGE
1 AMERICAN, 1 FRENCH CANADIAN, 24/26 JUNE
Capt. Maniere, Sgt. Durocher

The date of their despatch had been changed to June, but throughout the report Maniere suggests, May, but this is likely due to the time elapsed before the report was written.

This small team landed to reinforce Team Veganin, they were met by around 30 men. Some reception committees were small, others numbered far higher. The radio operator was ultimately left in the Vercors to assist.

Capt. Maniere tells of a German plane shot down and the pilot captured by the Maquis and transported to Vercors, where a hotel was used to imprison captured enemy. The Germans then arrived in a village near the crash site and without warning opened fire, killing around 60 civilians, women hanging out their washing, others just walking down the street, completely indiscriminately. They warned if their airman was not returned they would return in a few days and destroy the village. The airman was not returned and they did not return.

Unfortunately Capt. Maniere was eventually captured and imprisoned, he suffered verbal and psychological abuse but survived. The radio operator, makes clear in his report that he wants to go home to Canada on leave before considering any further missions, he managed to leave the Vercors before the German attack. He does confirm the drop date as June not May.

EPHEDRINE
2 FRENCH, 1 AMERICAN, 12/13 AUGUST
Lt. Donnart, Lt. Swank, Lt. Desplechin

Dropped in just a day before Fred and Team Citroën, the first pages of their report deals with the tragic accidental shooting of Lt. Swank. They were travelling with a number of people in a truck, and having stopped to stretch their legs, Lt. Donnart's rifle which was not on him at the time, accidentally discharged and shot Lt. Swank. Despite the efforts of the Resistance doctor, he could not be saved.

The remaining members of the team continued with their mission and were effective in providing explosives and arms for the Maquis. They reported atrocities across several villages and named the German who was responsible for ordering for these crimes. They eased off due to the reprisals but the Germans continued. They attempted to get American reinforcements but could not. They continued and with the aid of Maquis and poor weather were at least able to hasten the Germans' departure, but substantial infrastructure damage was caused by the departing Germans. The team highlighted that a lack of information from High Command hindered their efforts, as well as organisational issues from the Jeds. In spite of the tragic loss of one of the team, they remained focused and determined so were able to have a very positive impact.

GRAHAM
1 BRITISH, 2 FRENCH, 1 AMERICAN 12/13 AUGUST
Major Crosby, Capt. Gavet, Sgt Adams

Sgt Adams did not go into the field; for some reason it was planned that he would join them later. The two remaining members of the team initially found themselves in Corsica awaiting transport, then Crosby was recalled to Algiers before being returned. Ultimately the two men were then transported to Italy before going into France, dates seem confused. The report states 12/13 August but Crosby states it was 8/9 August.

There seems to have been the usual difficulty in contacting the right people on the ground, but they found good men who needed training. They co-ordinated with the Maquis and then the Americans and were involved in Apt, as was Team Citroën. They found themselves also having to dip into Italy to avoid the Germans, but were able to fool the Germans into thinking there were more of them than there were. It seems even villagers assisted them in attempting to convince Germans that sheep on far-off ridges were in fact Allied troop reinforcements. They commented that the Americans simply did not believe in the Free French fighters and that lost time for all. The usual 'too late' argument was also made.

JEREMY
2 BRITISH, 1 FRENCH, 16/17 AUGUST
Capt. Lt Giese, Sgt. Leney

The team report contradicts the despatch date stating it was 24/25 August. They were dropped to the Haute Loire region and Capt. Hallowes set off for Le Puy after a day, leaving the radio operator to set up at a Maquis hideout. They reported good numbers of Maquis, but not well organised. They also reported how many men had suddenly jumped on the bandwagon of the Resistance and elevated their positions by placing Major badges on themselves. This was an issue in the final throes of the war; many good men and women had worked tirelessly and in great danger for years yet some threw themselves forward at the last minute making false claims about their involvement. This naturally led to ill will and a reluctance to deal with these 'new majors'. The team found the FTP uncooperative and rude, so did not arm them as they were not willing to take orders from anyone other than their own commanders. The team was able to arm and train hundreds of men who were ready and willing to halt any German movement through the area. They also organised them into companies, ensured transport for them and wanted to move them north and east to harass the departing Germans. By 7 September they had organised the Maquis and ensured each company had adequate arms and transport. The French member of the team worked to ensure that a number of recent 'majors' were left in Le Puy and that the team could continue unhindered. They continued to assist the Maquis, although they said obtaining petrol was a great difficulty. The team report ends with them continuing to the Vosges to aid the Maquis with mopping up. The report is dated 16 September, but also shows that they did not return from France until the last week of October.

The radio operator, Leney, states that all worked well and gave his thanks to base for their speedy response when necessary.

Roger Leney was a friend of Fred's and they enjoyed meeting up decades later at reunions. Hallowes would marry Odette, the famed SOE agent. She would be one of several to threaten libel action when M R D Foot's history of SOE was first published in the mid 1960s. Having not been allowed to speak to any of those involved with SOE, there were many errors and much misinformation which Foot was required to correct at least partially. This did not help with the myths surrounding the service.

JOHN
2 BRITISH, 1 FRENCH, 16/17 AUGUST
Capt. Stern, Lt Comte M de Galbert, Sgt. Gibbs

The drop was not too bad, the slipstream caused some severe twisting and the group's pannier dropped without a parachute. In the words of the team's official report, items including their carbines changed shape drastically due to the impact. An inexperienced ground reception, who were not expecting them, meant that it took some minutes to suddenly become clear that the team were in the Ariege area, around 150 kilometres from their intended area. Team Chrysler had apparently landed nearby. They were moved to a farm and told to lie low, the following day they were told that the locals would see what they could do but that moving north might be difficult. A few days later they were able to move in spite of some tension between Spanish and Maquis groups. They were not able to locate their contact but came across a well-organised if ill-equipped Maquis group and decided to help them. They then joined a 1,500-strong column of Maquis heading south with Jedburgh Teams Mark, Miles and Martin. They comment on the smartness and discipline of these Maquis and how well organised they were. They mention the leader, Capt. Parizot, as being a fine soldier who was tragically killed on 6 September. They settled in Toulouse to assist with the recovery of a German aircraft and to aid wounded and sick and arrange their transport out.

They were disappointed not to have done more, as they state the astoundingly bad navigation which saw them dropped in completely the wrong region, coupled with an inability to reach their contact, made them feel that their mission was hopeless from the start. In spite of this, they did complete good work, aiding and training Maquis and simply being there was a morale boost for those who had felt so alone for so long. Again they commented on being sent in too late.

MARK
1 FRENCH, 2 AMERICANS,16/17 AUGUST
Lt. De Thevenet, Lt. Conein, Sgt. Carpenter

The team could see the drop zone clearly as they came over it, however, the pilot headed into the wind meaning the team landed 6 km from the site and one member suffered a sprained ankle, no doubt caused by the pilot also not slowing down. They managed after a day to make contact with Hilaire, George Starr, who arranged a meeting with the local Maquis leaders. Orders were given that the team could not move without approval from one of the local leaders. This was bypassed when a German column began moving through the area and Hilaire told them to use their position (they were uniformed and carrying a letter from Eisenhower). A battle ensued. Delays caused by inexperience in the Maquis and their desire, against the team's wishes, for an armistice, meant that the battle lasted longer than it should. They returned to Toulouse where there was fighting in the streets, Lt. Conein was withdrawing when his car broke down and he was mobbed and fired upon; he advised that the Americans were coming and that he was simply the advance party. The team were then employed in a political/military role, with the French member of the team fully involved in secret meetings. At one point Lt Conein went to the Spanish border and reported back on the Germans escaping to Spain and many Spaniards coming into France. The team's mission switched during this time to one of intelligence. They were finally stood down and sent to Paris in mid November.

MARTIN
2 BRITISH, 1 FRENCH, 16/17 AUGUST
Capt. Mellows, Lt. Redonnet, Sgt. Carey

Dropped to the Wheelwright circuit in the Gers region, Capt. Mellows was killed and no team report exists. Nonetheless we know they were involved with Teams Mark, Miles and John as previously described. See Team Miles' report for details of Capt. Mellows death. Carey returned to England at the end of September 1944 with the French officer Remond returning in January 1945.

MASQUE
2 AMERICANS, 1 FRENCH, 27 AUGUST
Capt. Guillot, Lt. Bouvery, Sgt. Poche

Despatched to the Isere region to be at the disposal of Commandant Noir. Due to German movements around the Rhône it was deemed both risky and time-consuming to track the Commandant down and instead the team put themselves at the disposal of the local Maquis leader. They were instrumental in assisting in the liberation of Lyon, organising the Maquis groups' routes and itinerary. They felt that they should have been dropped in months beforehand to assist and organise. They also felt that far more men and equipment could have been dropped in to them without incident. Nevertheless, they commended both their training and the interaction they had in France. They commented on the discipline and organisation of the Free French which they felt was superior to the FTP.

MILES
2 AMERICANS, 1 FRENCH, 16/17 AUGUST
Capt. Allen, Lt Esteve, Sgt. Gruen

Another team dropped to the Wheelwright circuit, to operate in the Gers region. The team joined a group of 600 Maquis and participated in action near Auch. They were with Team Martin and left with them towards the town of Mont-de-Marson, where they heard that Germans were involved in demolitions. The next day they entered the town, the Germans having fled overnight. Following news of another German column approaching they set about checking the town's defences. Sadly as they were checking one area, the Germans appeared and began firing, Capt. Mellows of Team Martin was hit - he had suffered an ankle injury during his jump and was unable to get away. Capt. Allen and Capt. Fourcade were able to escape to the woods. When the maquis located Capt. Mellows body, he had been hit by machine-gun fire in the stomach and chest, and he also had been shot by the Germans with 4 bullets in his head from his own gun. The battle for the town lasted 5 hours, with both sides withdrawing, the Germans suffered more losses than the Maquis but the loss of Capt. Mellows was deeply felt. The team withdrew to Toulouse as requested by Hilaire, they encountered sporadic fighting which they state they repulsed with little effort. They then moved south-east to Villepouche, the Germans having rushed through the area, the team assisted in rounding up Milice and collaborators. They then moved on to Narbonne, mopping up small groups of Germans, Milice and collaborators. They also went to Port Vendres to check the harbour which was in the process of being rebuilt. After that they checked the Maquis group at Perpignan, suggesting they were a little weak and ill-prepared to deal with the 'tickly' Spanish question on the border. After this they returned to Toulouse.

The team criticise Hilaire for meddling politically. They state he was not military and credit should be given to his teams for their military successes rather than him. They state the number of military missions in the city caused unnecessary problems with mixed messages and orders from all directions. This combined with Hilaire's meddling in Toulouse meant that when De Gaulle arrived, all Allied missions were ordered out.

MINARET
1 BRITISH, 1 AMERICAN, 9 JULY
Major Hartley-Sharpe, Capt. Cros (not deployed), Sgt. Ellis

The third member of this team did not go in due to illness, whether this was the illness which had affected a good number of those in Algiers is unknown. The team were despatched to Barre des Cevennes with the aim of arranging the mass surrender of Armenian troops. Unlike most other teams they were not intended to engage with the Maquis. They made contact with British mission and Commandant Jean, known as Isotrope and the Major stayed with them for several days while Ellis was moved to a safe house to set up communications. The team decided to move to L'Osporou to meet up with the Aiguel Maquis group, but they had already moved on. Ellis stayed here with good support from Maquis while Sharpe moved down to Vellerogue.

Ellis briefly joined him but the location in a deep valley was not suited to radio communications. Sharpe was able to arrange the surrender of over 160 Armenian troops and assisted in organising sabotage efforts on the Gagos/Vellerogue road, both a tunnel and bridge being attacked. The report states that the Maquis were non-political but had achieved little until the Jed team arrived. They were then inspired and eager to do anything possible and the team assisted them. They determined to liberate the town of Lasalles with support from the team. Ellis got a little lost en route and then broke down in Dunfort, but he overcame the suspicions of the locals and was able to be towed to Lasalles. Sharpe briefly returned to Vellerogue before returning and assisting Ellis in finding a reasonable location for the radio; communications had been difficult due to both enemy action and the local terrain. A brief stay in Lasalles was followed by the team travelling with the Maquis to St Hyppolite de Fort, where the Germans mounted strong resistance. Sharpe made contact with the Germans and they surrendered in large numbers. There were around 1800 prisoners taken, and 300 dead, the Maquis suffered 25 losses. This is a fine example of the soldier/diplomat role of the Jeds. The team travelled swiftly from here, arriving in Nimes a few days before the French Army arrived. They made contact with various Maquis groups but they were communist and there was political friction in the area.

At this point they felt the mission was at an end; few enemy were still in the area and there were no Armenians in the area. Yet while there they helped to process 1400 prisoners of war. They specify their time in Nimes as mostly social, with reference to considerable celebrations and state it was a tearful farewell as they said goodbye to the Maquis and headed for Vals, which despite being only a few kilometres away took some time due to blown bridges. At this point they made contact with Colonel Chassy, Major Jordan, Major Murk, Major Grenville, Sgt. Cornick and Cynthia Turnbull who acted as liaison for Maquis groups and acted as a driver for the team. Again a short social stay before heading to Lyons with Major Grenville. Once in Lyons, the team was shut down and handed equipment and coding equipment to SFU4 there. They spent a few days sorting out equipment and no doubt socialising. Sharpe then decided to head to Marseille, but was actually heading to Italy to No.1 Special Force. He was delayed as the car he was going to travel in with Cynthia Turnbull, who was also heading to Italy, had been stolen. Another car was obtained and Sharpe left. Ellis reported to SFU4 asking for transport to Grenoble, where he understood other Special Forces were situated. Instead he was directed back to England, via Paris, which was not altogether straightforward as he had no papers. He got a flight back to England but was met by an intelligence officer who was suspicious of him. He headed back to Devonshire Close to report in, but being a weekend, he had to wait until Monday.

There were two detailed reports in the file, one written by the radio operator, states they did a useful job. They were like too many dropped too far away from their original drop site and of course the inevitable complaint of being dropped in too late. Special mention is made of the RAF who dropped them in, who were all lost over the Spanish border after safely dropping them. They could not praise the Maquis highly enough.

MONOCLE
2 AMERICANS, 1 FRENCH, 13/14 AUGUST
Previously discussed.

NOVOCAINE
2 AMERICANS, 1 FRENCH, 6/7 AUGUST
Lt. Gennerich, Lt. Pronost, Sgt. Thompson

The team dropped to a mountain plateau near Seyne les Alpes, with the reception team expecting someone else. The team spent the first few days instructing the Maquis in the use of their guns. They were then instructed to cut the route the Germans were taking and were ordered to Vallouise. Unfortunately this meant abandoning most of their equipment and supplies, which was far from ideal. It took two days to travel in the back of a truck. They stopped near Guillestre where they met their mission group and explained the plans. They also picked up two South African soldiers who had been Italian prisoners of war, then released and had fought with Italian partisans before heading into France. It is noted that they were a great help. Having left much of their supplies behind they had to steal one and a half tons of French black powder and they also decided to cut the water supply to the German garrison at Guillestre.

They carried out a recce on the roads south of Briancon, checking on a bridge, tunnel and secondary road. During this time they realised they were being observed and captured two Frenchmen working for the Germans, who were despatched to the Maquis camp. An overnight operation saw them demolish a bridge, a tunnel and cut a secondary road. Back in Guillestre the Maquis attacked the Germans, as well as cutting their water supply. Team Chloroform had cut their communications to the west and a surrender to the allies was organised by Team Novocaine and Major Purvis, Capt. Roper and some FFI officers. The team went on to assist with cutting the Grenoble-Briancon road. They came under attack while at Prelles, while there was little effect on them, they reported the wanton killing of civilians and burning of houses by German troops. After this the team made contact with advancing Americans and requested assistance. A recce was made on Briancon and it found that the Germans had left; a defence was set up. Germans then attacked the town, they were comprised of German and Italian SS and Afrika Korps. The colour of the Afrika Korps uniform led to them initially being mistaken for Americans by the locals. The team requested more arms, but only received ammunition, but it was very welcome. The Americans withdrew leaving a small number of Maquis and the Jeds to hold the position. They managed this for 2 days until French Forces arrived to reinforce. It took 2 days to take the town after which the team considered their job done and reported to Grenoble.

Their final report comments on the rank of those dropped in, they encountered problems as they were of a lower rank than many in the Maquis and persuading them to do what the team required was unnecessarily difficult due to this issue. The Maquis promoted in the field and towards the end of the war as other teams found, many simply stuck major badges on and started handing out orders. They found the rank and file of the Maquis willing but often the leaders did not want to endanger themselves so the team had to take command. The rank issue also impacted the radio operator, as we know all were moved to Sergeant status, but his was a lowly rank in the field with the Maquis and the radio operator encountered problems. Messages and requests for equipment were often ignored, from their perspective. Of course they also comment that they should have been sent in earlier.

PACKARD
1 AMERICAN, 2 FRENCH, 31 JULY
Capt. Bank, Lt Denis, 2/Lt. Montfort

The original radio operator for the team was replaced with Hontfort from the French Army who was not a Jedburgh.

Dropped to the Lozere department and met by the Allied mission, their role was to carry on guerrilla activities whether the mission was in agreement or not. They stayed with the mission for a few days where they encountered the local FTP leader, described as a rabid communist. The mission ordered the team to give the FTP their arms which they reluctantly did on the promise of a future drop of arms. They planned with the FTP a regime of sabotage, the team assisted with the more complicated destructions. They were successful in ensuring the destruction of critical road bridges and blocking rail tunnels as well as cutting rail lines in the Gard. There was also mining of roads, cutting phone lines and destruction of pylons across both the Lozere and Gard departments. They then met with the FFI leader in the region and found him excellent; there was sustained sabotage taking place under his command. The FFI also captured trains with food supplies and distributed to the local population, although one load was stolen by the FTP - highlighting the countrywide issue between differing Resistance factions.

The team established a training school for demolitions split between the Communists and the other resistance groups. Three hundred Armenians deserted the Germans around this time and joined the FTP and proved very useful. They welcomed Team Minaret into the field who left as previously described to assist the Aigual Maquis.

The team prepared for the anticipated move of German forces with both factions of the Maquis well equipped and ready for action. The Germans retreated from Ales and the Resistance forces moved in, two days later the city was fully liberated. Constant fighting continued on the road between Ales and Uzos. They lost around 600 from the FTP when they decided to go to Nimes without warning for political reasons, which had the knock-on effect of making the FFI send men there as well. This weakened their previously good fighting force. While cooperation was difficult they were able to regularly send messages and the RAF were very efficient strafing in their area. They were in a difficult position, in flat open land and losses were mounting on the Resistance side as Germans came through their position by the thousand. They left for the French forces at Tarascon to try to get some additional support. They had to nip through the enemy columns and row across the Rhône and reported to Divisional headquarters before heading back through enemy lines to Ales. A few days later the Germans had pretty much completed their retreat through the area with the French forces arriving too late. The team, having reported to Grenoble, then went to Briancon to assist along with Team Novocaine in the attack and occupation. The team also drew up a plan of the location of Lt. Swank's (Team Ephedrine) grave and a photo was taken and reported to the graves registration officer.

The team's report states that they never received any drops and that this put them in a difficult position with the Resistance forces, whom they had promised weapons to. Also it seems the mission had promised the arms they dropped with to the FTP; they should have been advised of this before departure. The French officer of the team made the points that the Isotrope Mission favoured the communists, who were less effective or interested than the FFI. Also they tried to hold the Jeds back while not knowing their own priorities, but not wanting the Jeds to steal their thunder. They comment that while German prisoners of war were well treated by the Resistance forces, the Milice prisoners were shot as were some collaborators. Of course the comment that they should have been sent in earlier was made.

QUININE
2 BRITISH, 1 FRENCH, 8/9 JUNE
Major Macpherson, Lt Le Prince M de Bourbon-Parme, Sgt. Brown

The team were dropped to the Lot area near Cahors to assist the Maquis particularly along the Montauban/Brive communication line.

They dropped to the arranged drop zone to find a small number of poorly-armed men. Those on the ground had never heard of the contact they were supposed to meet. There was heavy movement of Germans and the team was able to locate a small Maquis group south of Correze, arming them and assisting them in delaying the enemy's progress, through blowing up a bridge, mounting multiple dummy ambushes and ultimately delaying the enemy by defending a bridge for six hours, although of the 27 men who took part in this action, 20 were killed. The team then focused on their original plan. Finding excellent Maquis in Lot, they managed to stop all rail traffic between Cahors and Souillac. The road was more difficult but they trained the Maquis in ambushes which worked perfectly.

Having completed this operation, they realised with few Germans in their area, there was a need for more co-ordination across a larger area. They travelled widely and were able to instigate the cutting of the railway network in over 600 locations using those already in place. They continued to train the Maquis during this time. As the southern invasion approached, they were in contact with Resistance leaders throughout the area, offering intelligence and assistance. As large numbers of enemy troops moved east, the team was asked to help form a mobile FFI force, which totalled 22,000 men, they report that the force worked well, capturing more than their own number of prisoners.

The first item in the official file was not the team's report but a letter written by Macpherson. He complains vehemently about a report in the *Times* newspaper which claims an American lieutenant using just 20 men captured 20,000 Germans. It was an incorrect report which Macpherson demanded be corrected. This surrender was precipitated by the team's action as well as the FFI with the surrender being made to the team and the FFI. He argues that this misrepresentation damages already fragile relations in central

France. He reports that American flags were torn down and burned, clearly antagonising locals who had endured enough with German occupiers and certainly did not want the American flag replacing the Swastika. This resentment against the liberators was often due to the FFI and other Resistance groups not receiving due credit for the sacrifices they made and the contribution they made in freeing their own country. This misrepresentation was widely covered in the French media and did nothing for relations between the Allies and France. Macpherson suggested the Americans could bestow some awards on the French colonels, but was told that was impossible but letters of appreciation were promised but had not been given. The Americans had apparently acknowledged the truth in a short paragraph in the Stars and Stripes news.

It seems that Macpherson wrote several reports, not shown in the team's file. It is fair to say that he felt strongly that the Americans wrongly attempted to claim victories that were in fact French victories. This was a team which went in relatively early compared to others and were clearly very effective, but whose efforts like so many were simply swept aside.

SCEPTRE
Previously discussed

SCION
2 BRITISH, 1 FRENCH, 29/30 AUGUST
Major Grenfell, Lt. Gruppo, Sgt. Cain

This team was originally called Joseph and was destined for the Lot region of France. However, they were dropped with Team Masque into the Ardeche region. Their only incident on landing was that the French team member landed some distance away and was almost shot as he did not know the password. As with Team Masque they had to decide whether to cross the Rhône or put themselves at more local disposal. Given the rapid retreat of the Germans and the speedy advance of the Americans they decided to offer their services more locally. They were offered the chance to head south where the Resistance were getting to grips with 3000 Germans. The hope was to liberate Lyon, however, in spite of good numbers of Maquis a day of delays meant the Germans had left by the time they entered the city. Nonetheless there were several days of street fighting as the Milice continued to fight. As good as the Maquis were, they were ill-trained for street fighting and unfortunately some of their own were killed by friendly fire. The team worked well in a liaison role and reconnaissance but were disappointed not to be utilised more, the only real action seems to have been the two days in Lyons where they felt they were simply plain soldiers, although they comment that their car was hit by machine-gun fire, so it wasn't an easy two days. They felt it was difficult arriving so late which caused some mistrust. Their radio operator was loaned to the Resistance and did an excellent job for them. They questioned their months of waiting in Algiers when they could have been achieving so much in France. They did comment that the idea of an Allied team was excellent and worked well. The report ended stating the team was willing and able for any mission anywhere.

VEGANIN
2 BRITISH, 1 FRENCH, 8/9 JUNE
Major Marten, Capt. Vuchot, Sgt. Gardner

This team was heading to the east bank of the Rhône. Sadly Sgt. Gardner, a good friend of Fred's, was killed on the jump in. The parachute did not open and it looked as if the hook had not been well pinned to the aircraft. Their initial reception was very cordial but the search for containers took some time and during the search the body of Gardner was found by Major Marten which was obviously a blow to all. Not all containers or packages were found and the radios were smashed as the parachutes had not opened. They were transported to a small house where they stayed. Gardner was initially buried wrapped in his parachute and placed in a container. He would later be reburied with honours at Beaurepaire.

The remaining team members stayed in the area for several days before being transported to meet a Maquis chief. This chap apparently exaggerated the numbers of troops he had, but he and others were all very enthusiastic. They needed arms and political differences between groups in the area were clearly an issue with FTP joining other groups but not following orders, simply doing as they wished. It was seriously suggested to the groups that they split into FTP and Armee Secret given the political issues. The team found themselves embroiled in the politics despite instructions. The invasion in Normandy provoked a general insurrection, but the Germans retaliated, killing and burning farms. In St Donat, they looted, raped women and took hostages yet were not keen to engage with the Maquis. Ongoing political problems caused the team to gather all the units which had a political mix together and offered the FTP members the opportunity to split and return to pure FTP units, which they did. This did not solve all the problems, a lack of arms, the slow advance of the allies meant that many Maquis simply went home. This was a very difficult period for the team as the Maquis dissolved in front of them. As disappointing as this was for the team they had some sympathy for those who had waited for so long and had so little in terms of arms or support but who saw such brutal reprisals. They wanted to be rid of the Germans but were going to wait until they had sufficient arms and reinforcements before engaging in any sabotage or ambush. The team attempted to train and organise some sabotage but the Maquis left were not interested and attempts to sabotage the railway failed.

The SOE agent for the area reported that his men thought very highly of the team and that they did a magnificent job in harassing the enemy retreat in what was an extremely difficult and dangerous sector.

WILLYS
2 BRITISH, 1 FRENCH, 28/29 JUNE
Capt. Marchal, Capt. Montague, Sgt. Cornick

Dropped to the Ardeche area and placed under the Allied mission run by French Commandant Vanel. They were to help the military side of the Resistance however encountered strong resistance from the mission and it's staff. The radio operator worked well but for mission, the French member of the team was put to work on intelligence, in spite of their already being an excellent officer in charge of that. Captain Montague found himself somewhat cast aside. All suggestions and recommendations were ignored. He attempted under his own steam to visit Maquis groups and found them eager and willing but their command in terms of Vanel and others were unwilling and disinterested. He was successful in encouraging some blowing of bridges and road blocks, but all requests for equipment went unanswered. He did what he could in terms of advising but found the various Maquis groups had no regular system of contact with their command and there was no leadership. Montague felt so much more could have been done and sooner had there been better command on the ground of the Maquis and had the Jed team been able to do what they had been trained to do. He commented that not only did he receive no help from the mission but they were hostile and attempted to exclude him. Supplies were generally bad, either never arriving or were insufficient with multiple incidents of chutes not opening on containers so damaged or destroyed contents. In fact one container killed a member of the Maquis when its parachute failed to open. He said this hostility extended to the Americans and whether it was nationalistic or personal he was unsure, but he was glad that he managed to do a little with the support of the local Maquis groups.

There's an overriding theme in the reports, that they were sent in too late. Nonetheless, it's important not to fixate on this as many have done. So many teams did so much good, which many of them dismissed. The simple act of their presence with letters from Koenig were a huge morale boost for the Resistance. So many teams took part in action, but their very demeanour meant that they often dismissed their efforts as nothing of importance. Every one of them made an impact, either personally on those they interacted with and in the contribution they brought, either training, advising and being involved in actions on the ground. For some, like Team Willy, it was frustrating and they were clearly under-utilised, yet still contributed, perhaps not in the way or as much as they wanted but they did what they could.

For others, including Fred, they saw some action but always downplayed it. Captain Smallwood of Fred's team said, nothing much happened, yet they were involved in multiple skirmishes and incidents, any one of which could have killed them.

OTHER TEAMS DROPPED TO FRANCE - As these teams are not directly relevant to Fred or the south of France, details have been kept brief. Some reports are written in French and for the purposes of this work have not been fully translated.

ALAN
2 FRENCH, 1 BRIT, 13 AUGUST
   Dropped to assist the Resistance and harass the enemy particularly on the road and rail network around Lyons/Nevers and Lyon/Dijon. The team had ongoing problems as their Jed set broke on landing, so they had to improvise. They relocated the Maquis groups and trained them to carry out effective sabotage.

ALASTAIR
2 BRITS, 1 FRENCH, 28 AUGUST
   Dropped to assist the FFI and provide a link between London and the FFI in the region. Vosges area north-east of St Die. The reception committee the team dropped to was 500 strong and expecting more arms than the team had. The radio operator on one occasion came across a German soldier who asked him for a light, he duly obliged and carried on. The team had a few close encounters like this.

ALEC
2 AMERICANS, 1 FRENCH, 9/10 AUGUST

To accompany SAS team to Loire et Cher and to be a link between the SAS and the Resistance. Dropped 60 miles east of the area for which they were briefed. The team found themselves within the main corridor being used by Germans to evacuate east. The Maquis did a good job and the team assisted both with bridge-blowing and liaising with advancing troops.

ALEXANDER
2 AMERICANS, 1 FRENCH, 12/13 AUGUST

Dropped in the area of Creuse with instructions to accompany a half troop of SAS. Organise and provide equipment to the Resistance. Harass enemy movements by road and rail between Perigeux-Limoges-Chateauroux and Toulouse-Limoges-Chateauroux. The team found themselves in a different area to the one they expected, and commented on the nervy situation every time they crossed a major road, due to the numbers of Germans around. They comment that their most important work was around the German V 4 weapon. The were able to obtain the plans for this weapon and forward them to Paris.

ALFRED
2 BRITS, 1 FRENCH, 24/24 AUGUST

Despatched to the Oise area to assist the organisation of the FFI and to provide a link between London and the FFI in the area to facilitate equipment drops. The team struggled to get supplies but took part in some ambushes with the Maquis.

ANDREW
2 BRITS, 1 BELGIAN, 15/16 AUGUST

Dropped to the Ardennes area, they were to assist the FFI and assist in organising stores to the Resistance. They were to contact Citronelle circuit. The team were split on their drop and it took some time for them to get together, fortunately at a friendly farm. They were involved in various battles in their area.

ANDY
2 BRITS, 1 FRENCH, 11/12 JULY

Dropped to the Haute Vienne region, a very bad drop resulted in injuries to two of the team - one a broken leg and the French team member a badly damaged foot. The injured men were evacuated back to England after a relatively short spell in France.

ANTHONY
2 AMERICANS, 1 FRENCH, 15 AUGUST

Dropped to Saone et Loire to provide liaison between SAS and local Resistance and London. To assist in harassing enemy movements. They dropped with some SAS troops. They found the immediate need was for action. Had they gone in earlier they could have helped train more Maquis.

ARCHIBALD
1 BRIT, 1 AMERICAN, 1 FRENCH, 25/26 AUGUST

Dropped to Meurthe and Moselle region, to assist the FFI and provide a link between London and the Resistance in the area.

Such was the effectiveness of both the Resistance and the Jed team that the Germans estimated there were 20 Allied officers and 2000 well armed men, when if fact there was the Jed team of three and 300 armed men as well as 250 who were not armed.

ARNOLD
2 BRITS, 1 FRENCH, 24/25 AUGUST

Dropped to the Marne area, to co-ordinate with the FFI and provide a link between them and London to ensure supplies. Also to liaise with SOE circuits in the area. A loss of radio meant difficulties, this team was sent in wearing civilian clothes but had no papers, meaning difficulties. They managed to liaise between Maquis groups and the advancing American troops.

ARTHUR
2 AMERICANS, 1 FRENCH, 18/19 AUGUST

Dropped to the Cote d'Or area, to co-ordinate with the FFI and provide a link with London to ensure supplies. American Captain injured spine due to parachute issue. They complained that requests for arms went unanswered and did not help with relations with the Maquis.

AUBRY
2 BRITS, 1 FRENCH, 11/12 AUGUST

A standard aim to assist the FFI and provide a link to London. Dropped to the Seine et Marne area, the first Jed team to be dropped in civilian clothes, they flew from Harrington. This team headed into Paris, where they witnessed street fighting and reprisals against those who tried to fly the French flag. They reported busy restaurants with no issues relating to food supply although prices were high. The team returned to their original location but the Germans located there for a while which made life difficult, the team leader at one point having to take refuge in a lake for over eight hours, he survived in spite of the Germans firing on the lake. The French member of the team, Telmon, was killed in action.

AUGUSTUS
2 AMERICANS, 1 FRENCH, 15/16 AUGUST

Dropped to the Aisne area, it began as the standard operation, assist the FFI and provide a link to London.

The Jed team Augustus was completely wiped out, having dropped just a day after Fred and team Citroen further south. They dropped in the north, but having made contact with Allied troops attempted to cross the lines in order to carry on harassing the German rear line and ran straight into a German checkpoint during a dark and rainy night. They knew their papers would get them through but an inquisitive soldier started poking around the cart they were riding in, which under the hay were stacked a reasonable amount of arms and ammunition. All were shot as they attempted to escape.

BASIL
1 BRITISH, 1 FRENCH, 1 AMERICAN, 25/26 AUGUST

Dropped to the Doubs area, to assist the FFI and provide a link to London. The drop was from only about 300 feet so too low, resulting in a broken finger for one team member and another being concussed. Having asked to check before take off that all items were aboard, they were assured they were. On landing they had no radio or personal kit and had just what they were wearing and their pistols.

BENJAMIN
1 BRITISH, 2 FRENCH, 20/21 AUGUST

Dropped to the Meuse area, to assist the FFI and provide a link to London. Issues at Fairfield on despatch did nothing for the morale of the team and a drop into a wooded area meant they spent several days attempting to gather up all the equipment dropped. Unfortunately many of the local Maquis were caught in a German operation, having been betrayed, which caused the team to move quickly. They were able to engage in multiple actions and were effective in providing information to the advancing Americans. They worked with Team Bernard.

BERNARD
2 BRITISH, 1 FRENCH, 20/21 AUGUST

The team went in with Team Benjamin, with issues around the drop which included parachutes stuck in trees and visible to the enemy. They moved some distance away and moved regularly, working with Team Benjamin and attempting to divide an area between them. Two members of the team were wounded in action and removed to hospital behind the Allies' advancing line.

BRIAN
2 BRITISH, 1 FRENCH, 27/28 AUGUST

Also dropped to the Doubs area, they were able to assess the Maquis in the area and assist. They took decisions on the ground to make the best use of their skills, liaising well with the local groups, but found obtaining arms for them very difficult. They were involved in several operations with the Maquis with the French team member being wounded in action.

BRUCE
2 FRENCH, 1 AMERICAN, 14/15 AUGUST

Deployed to the Yonne area to assist the FFI and provide a link to London and to contact the Donkeyman circuit. The team dropped into the middle of Montgargis, some 20 miles from the intended drop zone. Townsfolk were awoken to the sound of containers dropping around the town. Warned of a nearby German garrison the team fled the town without their radio or equipment. An ensuing storm meant they trudged through mud while connected to each other via their pistol lanyards. Eventually they came across a Resistance radio post and were able to gain assistance. The team's diplomatic skills were tested in dealing with various commanders in the area and they were restricted by having to share a radio but they worked to bring various groups together and distributed arms and their liaison work was valuable.

BUNNY
2 BRITISH, 1 FRENCH, 17/18 AUGUST

Deployed to the Haute Marne region, they had a good landing and positive experience with the reception committee. Unfortunately one day while travelling in a truck it was attacked and Capt. Radice was hit in the leg. When he was eventually seen by a doctor, the leg had to be amputated but an infection had set in and spread, he died as a result. As well as working with the Maquis the team also worked with a small SAS team, aiding in sabotage. On one such excursion Gerville was hit, it was thought he was dead but the team sent to recover his body found he had dragged himself into bushes, he was transported to hospital. In spite of this the team was able to organise several successful sabotage operations.

CECIL
2 BRITISH, 1 FRENCH, 25/26 AUGUST
Deployed to the Aube department. They had the usual Jed role of harrassing the enemy and assisting the Maquis.

CEDRIC
2 AMERICANS, 1 FRENCH, 27/28 AUGUST
Deployed to the Haute Saone area, one of the team suffered injury exiting the aircraft but overall a good flight and reception. Drops that never came and constant engagements with the Germans meant this team was busy yet successful. One team member suffered an injury but was able to continue.

DANIEL I
2 BRITISH, 1 FRENCH, 5/6 AUGUST
Dropped to the wrong location, but landing safely with friendly locals around, the team was able to relocate and offer some assistance to the incoming Americans. They reported that some Maquis were well trained and others not so much, but all were enthusiastic and morale was high. They were also initially imprisoned by the Americans who did not appreciate who they were. They were pulled out after only a week.

DESMOND
2 AMERICANS, 1 FRENCH, 4/5 SEPTEMBER
This team dropped with an operation group who parachuted in on the same night. The team assisted with liaison between the OG, the Maquis and advancing troops. Their very detailed report gives an idea of the level of going back and forth involved in attempting to get things moving.

DOUGLAS 1
2 BRITISH, 1 FRENCH, 5/6 AUGUST
Having had a failed drop on the night of the 5th from Fairford, the team tried again on the 6th from Keevil. The flight until arrival was uneventful, then enemy anti aircraft fire caused some chaos in the aircraft due to pitching, nevertheless the team reported a good drop. They dropped with an SAS team and appear to have struggled with getting supplies which impacted their position. The radio operator was wounded.

DOUGLAS II
1 BRITISH, 1 FRENCH, 1 AMERICAN, 15 SEPTEMBER

Consisting of two members of Douglas I, the team having found the initial location was under Allied control. They moved and were in a good position to assist, but as they had experienced on their previous mission, communications with London were non-existent and they were unable to be of much use, to the disappointment of the Allies on the ground and themselves.

FELIX
2 BRITISH, 1 FRENCH, 8/9 JULY

This team dropped to the north eastern coastal area, while the coast was well fortified they found well organised Maquis that they were able to assist. They, with the Maquis, were able to be very effective, whether in ambushes, attacks, capturing food and ammunition. Beyond this they were instrumental in holding back a column of 600-700 German parachutists. They did complain that not enough clothing and boots were sent in for the Maquis with the comment that you cannot ask men to fight in clogs being most striking.

FRANCIS
2 BRITISH, 1 FRENCH, 9/10 JULY

Dropped to the far west of Brittany, the team's drop found them landing in woodland. Unfortunately one team member was separated at this point and not found for four days. In the meantime, the remaining team members had organised the Maquis into three groups. They had the normal issues of insufficient arms and drops, but organised a number of Maquis groups. At one point they found themselves surrounded by 600 Germans in a town but managed to escape. Unfortunately while at a farm, Germans arrived, killing the farmer immediately and shooting one of the team, who while wounded was then shot. Several Maquis escaped, the radio operator hid in a river and was ultimately able to escape and find a Maquis group and after a few days was joined by the French member of the team. An SAS sergeant laid down his life during this to enable others to escape.

FRANK
2 BRITISH, 1 FRENCH, 27 SEPTEMBER

They found their initial location quiet. While Germans were in the area, insufficient arms meant it was a case of letting sleeping dogs lie. They moved on to another area and spent time there, moving on again when aircraft with supplies were arranged. These were distributed but they received information that the area was handed over and all supplies would now go through headquarters. One team member was admitted to hospital which delayed the team leaving the area.

FREDERICK
1 BRITISH, 1 FRENCH, 1 AMERICAN, 9/10 JUNE

This team comments that their HQ for the first week was under a tree. They make multiple comments about the assistance of the Maquis and name several who they consider should receive awards. They were involved in several firefights and on one occasion found themselves surrounded by 800 Germans and in their words by some miracle they escaped.

GAVIN
2 FRENCH, 1 AMERICAN, 11/12 JULY

Their area was north of Rennes, dropped with Team Guy who covered the area south of Rennes. Their mission was to locate suitable drop sites for both men and equipment with orders not to take any action until advised by London. There was much frustration due to being dropped well outside their intended area and well over a week wasted as they attempted to locate and make contact with relevant Maquis. They were able to acquire a car, but were stopped by a German patrol, fortunately they managed to get away as the Germans were perplexed and didn't seem to realise they had Allied troops in their sights.

GEORGE
2 FRENCH, 1 AMERICAN, 9/10 JUNE

Dropped to help establish an SAS base, they found friction between themselves and the SAS at the airfield before departure. They were able to defuse the situation somewhat and while confusion carried on when in France, ultimately they found the SAS unit, in their words, original with no rules or regulations. They worked well with them. Theirs is a colourful report, with multiple actions.

GEORGE II
2 FRENCH, 1 AMERICAN, 7 SEPTEMBER

A second mission for the above team saw them back in the field for over two months. They were to organise mobile patrols to find the enemy.

GERALD
2 AMERICANS, 1 FRENCH, 18/19 JULY

Despatched to organise the Resistance in the Morbihan area, one of the most interesting comments in their report is that the Jedburghs and SAS cannot work together. They state that the Jedburghs were far superior when it came to diplomacy, tact and organisation.

GILBERT
2 BRITISH, 1 FRENCH, 9/10 JULY

Dropped to the Finistere area to organise the Resistance. They commented on the patriotism of the communist resistance and their support of De Gaulle, they were French first said the report.

GILES
1 AMERICAN, 1 FRENCH, 1 BRITISH, 8/9 JULY

Despatched to the Finistere area to organise the Resistance. Discussed earlier.

GODFREY
2 AMERICANS, 1 FRENCH, 11/12 SEPTEMBER

Despatched to the Haut Rhin area, their departure had been delayed six times, due to the advancing American Army.

GREGORY
2 BRITISH, 1 FRENCH, 4/5 SEPTEMBER

Despatched to the Vosges area, the day after arriving the team was ambushed with two team members injured.

GUY
2 FRENCH, 1 BRITISH, 11/12 JULY

This team worked with Team Gavin, see above.

HAMISH
2 AMERICAN, 1 FRENCH, 12/13 JUNE

Despatched to assist Team Hugh, the drop was too low and the radio operator suffered two sprained ankles. They stated that when they arrived there were 200-300 men, 150 of whom were armed. When they left there were 3000 with another 1000 awaiting arms. They commented that once liberated, their popularity waned somewhat, although they were treated with courtesy.

HAROLD
2 BRITISH, 1 FRENCH, 15/16 JULY

Despatched to the Vendee area, the navigator made an error and one team member dropped into a bakery yard in the middle of a village, the others were on the edge of the village. Discussed earlier. They stayed on to carry out further training at the end of their mission.

HARRY
2 FRENCH, 1 BRITISH, 6/7 JUNE

Despatched to the Mount Morvan area they dropped with 2 SAS officers. They were to assist the SAS in setting up a base.

HENRY
2 AMERICANS, 1 FRENCH, 9 SEPTEMBER

Despatched to Belfort area, they said they were furious that their radio had been smashed on landing due to poor packing. Met by Team Brian, they felt they went in too late.

HILARY
2 FRENCH, 1 AMERICAN, 17/18 JULY

Despatched to the Finistere area, this Breton area was praised by the team. The drop in was ok but one team member, in their own words, gave their head a good bounce and was stunned for a couple of days. They felt they had a real mission and were glad to be alive at the end of it.

HORACE
2 AMERICANS, 1 FRENCH, 17/18 JULY

Another team despatched to the Finistere area, this was a very active area with Germans located in every town and village. The Maquis though were organised and welcomed the arrival of teams to assist them.

HUGH
2 FRENCH, 1 BRITISH, 5/6 JUNE

Despatched to the Chatelleraut-Chateauroux area, the team were busy. They were proud of their work; they captured a good number of prisoners and were able to disrupt the enemy. They would not comment on the brutality of the Gestapo, other than to say it was tedious.

IAN
2 AMERICAN, 1 FRENCH, 20/21 JUNE

Despatched to the Vienne area, to help organise and train Maquis in the south-west area of the department. They were to also arrange attacks on the Bordeaux-Tours and Bordeaux-Saumur lines. They managed to organise 6000 men and could have recruited more if arms had been available.

ISAAC
2 British, 1 French, 10/11 June

Deployed as part of a larger inter allied mission.

IVOR
1 FRENCH, 1 BRITISH, 1 AMERICAN, 6/7 AUGUST

Despatched to the southern Cher area, they were to coordinate with Team Hamish. The radio operator was killed during exit from the aircraft. The radio operator from Team Andy was brought in. Another team member accidentally shot himself during his exit from the aircraft, while the third team member sprained an ankle on exit from the aircraft. In spite of this the two remaining members of the team carried on and were successful in their mission of aiding the Maquis.

JACOB
2 BRITISH, 1 FRENCH, 12/13 AUGUST

The team was dropped to the Vosges area with an SAS team. They and the Maquis they were with were attacked on 17 August. French team member killed, two British taken prisoner, only the radio operator survived and this in spite of a 42-day march, sleeping in snow without cover or sufficient food.

JAMES
2 AMERICANS, 1 FRENCH, 10/11 AUGUST

Despatched to the Correze area, to the south-east of Limoges. They reported issues between the rival Maquis groups and the political issues. People approached the team to complain that some methods employed by the political factions were just as frightening as the Germans.

JIM
2 AMERICANS, 1 FRENCH, 15/16 SEPTEMBER

Despatched to the Ain, Jura, Doubs area. They found the Maquis organised and were able to distribute arms. They worked with forward elements of the Allies and worked as liaison, but ultimately ran out of things to do.

JOCK
2 BRITISH, 1 FRENCH, OPERATION CANCELLED

JUDE I AND II
2 BRITISH, 1 FRENCH, 14/15 AUGUST, 7/8 NOVEMBER

Despatched to the Rhône area for their first mission. They found a good number in the Maquis, but not many who were well-trained or armed. They worked on establishing field hospitals in appropriate locations. They were in a busy location and were able to send through intelligence from those passing through. Their second mission involved the team training at the École de Cadres in the same area, where they found the French just as enthusiastic as they had been in the field.

JULIAN
2 BRITISH, 1 FRENCH, 10/11 AUGUST

Despatched to the Indre et Loire area, initially held training for the Maquis. German movements meant they had to move a few times, but continued to train groups and co-ordinated action against the enemy. They comment on the deplorable impression given after the German surrender, with the Germans breaking conditions apparently aided by an American officer. There were also reports of German and American officers fraternising, which the team felt were unfortunate especially for Franco-American relations.

JULIAN II
3 FRENCH, 19 NOVEMBER

Despatched to the Haut Rhin area, the team had multiple personnel changes before finally leaving England. The team landed at Epernay and drove to Nancy. Due to the speed of the advancing troops, their original plan changed. They hoped to get to Colmar but were unable and settled in Strasbourg. The situation remained serious into the new year.

LEE
1 AMERICAN, 2 FRENCH, 9/10 AUGUST

Despatched to the Haute Vienne area, they were involved in the liberation of Limoges, where they describe the initial chaos and the fact that the inhabitants were out for blood, understandably, before moving on to continue engaging the retreating Germans who were heading north. They saw an aircraft crash and in spite of engaging the Germans were unable to reach it. The French team member was killed in action.

MAURICE
2 AMERICANS, 1 FRENCH, 31 AUG/1 SEPTEMBER

Despatched to the Jura area, this team's report includes a statement of its finances. All teams were sent in with money and this team show how they spent theirs. This team's report begins with possibly the most colourful of all despatches, which was unsuccessful. Their state of mind, they declared, was akin to a woman whose lover had left without saying goodbye. Their way of saying they went in too late. The team did eventually go in and were kept busy.

NICHOLAS
2 BRITISH, 1 FRENCH, 10 SEPTEMBER

Despatched to the Bussieres area, but arrived 50 kilometres away and met an SAS team who advised wtih action ongoing it was impossible for them to get to their original location. The first Maquis group they encountered appeared well organised, but were attacked causing the team to disperse. The second group they met had little leadership, but they found themselves in the midst of battles. They did eventually get to Bussieres and realised that they could have done much more if dropped correctly and earlier.

NORMAN
2 AMERICANS, 1 FRENCH, 27/28 AUGUST

Despatched to the Jura, the team found the Maquis with very good morale and they had been well equipped and trained by Team Albert. The team worked with the Maquis carrying out sabotage and other works. They spoke very highly of all the Maquis, both men and women, who worked hard.

PAUL
2 BRITISH, 1 FRENCH, 18/19 AUGUST

Despatched to the Cote d'Or area, the next day meeting up with Team Arthur and arranging a doctor for one of the American members of the team who was injured. They instructed the Maquis but found that they were disappointed at their late arrival as they wanted them to arrange arms earlier. They stated that the Maquis found their presence a great morale boost.

PHILLIP
2 AMERICANS, 1 FRENCH, 31 AUG/1 SEPTEMBER

Despatched to the Meurthe et Moselle area where they encountered Team Archibald. They worked throughout a busy area, moving frequently. Their radio had been destroyed and this impacted their abilities. The team's radio operator was separated during an encounter, but he is not listed among the dead, wounded or captured.

QUENTIN
2 BRITISH, 1 FRENCH, 27 SEPTEMBER

Despatched to the La Rochelle area by ship from Plymouth, met by members of Team George and Tony at Les Sables d'Olonne. The team took over a battalion and liaised with American troops. They engaged with the enemy on multiple occasions and carried out sabotage of rail lines. They organised substantial training.

RAYMOND
2 BRITISH, 1 FRENCH, 27 SEPTEMBER

As the team above, despatched to the La Rochelle area, one of four teams despatched by ship from Plymouth. Linked up with Team Harold and offered training in arms, including some German arms which were liberated from the enemy. Laid mines and after engagements then worked to clear to allow Allies through. Gathered information to pass back to the Allies.

RODERICK
2 AMERICANS, 1 FRENCH, 31 AUGUST/1 SEPTEMBER

Despatched to the Doubs department, the drop to a small zone found one team member land in an oak tree, only bruised though. Found some Maquis well-trained and armed and others requiring arms. They met up with Team Cedric and agreed locations for operations. In spite of moving regularly, their camp was attacked but they escaped and carried on with ambushes. They entered Besançon with American troops, with the team losing most of its equipment during the battle.

RONALD
2 AMERICANS, 1 FRENCH, 5/6 AUGUST

Despatched to Finistere area, they had an additional French officer who was going to act as radio operator when dealing directly with mission Aloes, they were unable to contact them by radio. They located close to Quimper and were engaged in the battle for the town. They had tried to persuade the Germans to surrender but they refused saying they would only surrender to the American Army.

SIMON
2 BRITISH, 1 FRENCH, 27 SEPTEMBER

Despatched to La Rochelle area by ship from Plymouth. The team merged with Team Tony and shared the work. They drove to Normandy and Paris to gather arms, not all of which were forthcoming and were also required to attend various marches in liberated towns. They located multiple graves of Allied servicemen and reported their locations. They stayed on to help train French troops.

STANLEY
2 BRITISH, 1 FRENCH, 31 AUGUST/1 SEPTEMBER

Despatched to Haut Marne area, as well as having 400 Maquis with them they also had the whole first regiment of France; formally pro Pétain they had joined the Maquis. Multiple ambushes were engaged with and the team found the Pétain troops very keen, although poorly led.

TIMOTHY
3 AMERICANS, 1 FRENCH, 11 SEPTEMBER

The team dropped to the Amiens area, with one team member breaking both ankles due to a bad drop. They made their way to Besançon, there was an attempt to send a couple of team members to Switzerland but repeated attempts failed. They seemed to have little direct engagement with the enemy but liaised with various French elements.

TONY
2 AMERICANS, 1 FRENCH, 17/18 AUGUST

Despatched to the Vendée area, they were to concentrate on the German garrison at La Rochelle.

Beyond the standard Jed complaint at being sent in too late is that communications were clearly an issue with requests not fulfilled in multiple situations which impacted both the work and the reputation of those on the ground.

All of the reports from these teams make interesting reading. It is clear from the above that the preconception often repeated that the teams consisted of one American, one British and one French were untrue and that particular misnomer should be put to rest.

TEAMS DEPLOYED TO HOLLAND
- CLARENCE
- CLAUDE
- CANCELLED - see Team Henry
- DANIEL II
- DICING
- DUDLEY
- EDWARD
- GAMBLING
- STANLEY II

JEDBURGH TEAM MEMBERS KILLED OR WOUNDED IN ACTION

The following is a list of the casualties suffered by the Jedburghs, all of which are tragic but the relatively low number is testament to these men. This has been taken from *The Short History of the Jedburghs* by Arthur Brown, a member of Team Quinine.

MEN KILLED IN FRANCE AND HOLLAND

NAME	NATIONALITY	TEAM	CIRCUMSTANCES
N Viguier -nom de guerre. P Angoulvent	French	Lee	Unknown but believed to have been killed
Sgt J E Austin	British	Dudley	Arrested Dec. 1944 in Holland, shot while in captivity.
Maj. Bonsall	American	Augustus	Killed with rest of team by German forces
Lt Boissarie	French	Jacob	Killed in action September 1944
Lt Bordes	French	Alec	Wounded in action September 1944, died in hospital at Bourges
Sgt Bourgoin	American	Ian	Killed in action August 1944
Maj. Brinkgreve	Dutch	Dudley	Killed in action March 1945, Holland
Capt. Chaigneau	French	Aubrey	Killed in action August 1944
Sgt Cote	American	Augustus	Killed with rest of team by German forces
Capt. Delwiche	French	Augustus	Killed with rest of team by German forces
Capt. Fouere	French	Simon	Not known but killed
Sgt Gardner	British	Veganin	Killed by failure of parachute to open June 1944

NAME	NATIONALITY	TEAM	CIRCUMSTANCES
Sgt Goddard	American	Ivor	Killed by failure of parachute to open August 1944
Capt. Gough	British	Jacob	Captured, prisoner in Gestapo camp. Killed November 1944
Lt Groenewoud	Dutch	Claude	Killed in action September 1944
Capt. Mellows	British	Martin	Died of wounds while in enemy hands August 1944
Maj. Ogden-Smith	British	Francis	Wounded in action and subsequently died July 1944
Capt Radice	British	Bunny	Wounded in action and subsequently died August 1944
Sgt Scott	American	Claude	Killed in action September 1944
Lt Swank	American	Ephredine	Killed in an accident August 1944
Capt. Vochot	French	Veganin	Not known but killed

MEN WOUNDED IN FRANCE AND HOLLAND

NAME	NATIONALITY	TEAM	CIRCUMSTANCES
Sgt Bassett	British	Bernard	Wounded in ambush, evacuated to 39 Evac hospital (American-run)
Capt Bazata	American	Cedric	Wounded but able to carry on
Capt Bennett	British	Gregory	Wounded in ambush September 1944, operated on at 95 Evac hospital and transferred to British hospital in Naples

APPENDIX

NAME	NATIONALITY	TEAM	CIRCUMSTANCES
Capt Besterbreutje	Dutch	Clarence	Wounded in action September 1944 but able to carry on
Capt Cannicott	British	Alan	Seriously wounded in action
Lt Costes	French	Archibald	Wounded in action September 1944
Cdt Cretin	French	Brian	Wounded in action September 1944
Maj Denning	British	Archibald	Wounded in action but able to carry on
Maj Forrest	British	Benjamin	Wounded in action but able to carry on
Lt Geminel	French	Bunny	Seriously wounded in action, admitted to Langres Hospital September 1944
Capt. Harcourt	British	Cinnamon	Broke both legs due to a bad drop August 1944
Lt Heyns	American	Timothy	Broke both ankles due to bad drop September 1944
Lt Kaminski	French	Benjamin	Wounded in ambush September 1944 but able to carry on
Capt. Mynat	American	Arthur	Fractured spine due to bad drop August 1944, evacuated a month later to 39 Evac hospital
Capt Nasica	French	Bernard	Seriously wounded in action August 1944 evacuated to 39 Evac hospital
Maj. Parkinson	British	Andy	Compound fracture of leg due to bad drop July 1944. Evacuated by Lysander
Capt Ragueneau	French	George II	Broken leg due to bad drop Sepember 1944. Able to carry on

NAME	NATIONALITY	TEAM	CIRCUMSTANCES
Capt. De Schonen		Gregory	Wounded in ambush, operated on at 95 Evac hospital before evacuated to French hospital in Naples
Lt Verhaeghe	Dutch	Clarence	Wounded in action September 1944
Cdt Vermeulen	French	Andy	Broken ankle due to bad drop July 1944

Very few were captured but four survived, which given that there were orders to shoot on sight is quite remarkable.

NAME	NATIONALITY	TEAM	CIRCUMSTANCES
Maj. Harcourt	British	Dicing	Captured 9 April 1945 Holland, liberated at the end of April 1945
Maj. Manierre	American	Dodge	Captured August 1944, liberated by Russians from Stalag Luft 1 May 1945 – suggesting they may have thought he was an airman
Sgt Seymour	British	Jacob	Captured August 1944. Liberated April 1945
Capt. Todd	American	Claude	Captured September 1944, escaped 1 May 1945, with American troops overrunning the area a few days later

While it is possible to clarify those Jedburghs killed or wounded in France or Holland, it has, for this work, only been possible to check British records for the Far East. Those working for the Americans and French have not been checked, but there were casualties.

MEN KILLED IN THE FAR EAST

NAME	NATIONALITY	TEAM	CIRCUMSTANCES
Sgt Colvin	British	Nation/Hart	Killed during take-off at Dum Dum Airport, India March 1945
Capt. Marchant	British	Nation/Hart	Killed in the above take-off
Capt. Vickery	British	Nation/Hart	Killed in the above take-off
Lt Shearn	British	Calf/Lynx	Killed in action May 1945, Burma

There are no listings for wounded in the Far East, many men succumbed to illness and injury but due to the location they had to carry on; some like Roger Leney were extricated briefly for treatment, but there does not appear to be a consistent list.

The language in so many of these reports is a delight for historians, but also shows the measure of those chosen for the Jedburghs; they all like Fred seem to have had little time for fools and nonsense.

BIBLIOGRAPHY

Bailey, F. (1988-2023). *Personal Communications*. [Verbal].
Bailey, F. (1990). Bailey, Frederick Arthur, (Oral History). [online] 11 Dec. Available at: https://www.iwm.org.uk/collections/item/object/80011495 [Accessed September 2023 - May 2024].
Cox, M. (n.d.). *Fred Bailey*. [online] Legasee. Available at: https://www.legasee.org.uk/veteran/fred-bailey/?fbclid=IwAR3PYvquS9s69Jal48JO0SX4tAC-WNIZyztEAlgPPiz4QkG5qsdk1wh425A [Accessed October 2023-October 2024].
Smallwood, John Edward St. Clair (1990) Oral History - online. Available at: https://www.iwm.org.uk/collections/item/object/80017198 (accessed November 2023)
NATIONAL ARCHIVES - numerous files were accessed, for ease just main file numbers are listed.
CO 323/922/45
HS1-10 & 11 Burma Operations, Malaya
HS6 Jedburgh Team Reports
HS7 -17-19 Jedburgh History
HS7, Force 136

ACADEMIC WORK

Gutjahr, Major Robert, *The Role of Jedburgh Teams in Market Garden*, Master of Military Art and Science, US Army and General Staff College, Fort Leavenworth, 2001
Irwin, Wyman W, *A Special Force: Origin and Development of the Jedburgh Project in support of Operation Overlord, 1991.* Master of Military Art and Science, U.S. Army Command and General Staff College, Fort Leavenworth
Jones, Benjamin, *Freeing France: The Allies, the Resistance, and the Jedburghs*, 2008, PhD, University of Kansas
Lewis, S J, *Jedburgh Operations in Support of the 12th Army Group, August 1944.* 1991, U.S. Army Command and General Staff College, Fort Leavenworth.

Rosner, Major Elliot, *The Jedburghs: Combat Operations conducted in the Finistere Region of Brittany, France from July - September 1944*, U.S. Army Command and General Staff College, Fort Leavenworth, 1990

UNPUBLISHED SOURCES
Brown, Arthur, *The Jedburghs: A Short History*, 1991
Leney, Roger, *Mongoose White, Behind Enemy Lines in Burma*, 2005 - Courtesy of Simon Leney

BOOKS
Allen, Louis, *Burma, The Longest War 1941-45*, London: Phoenix Press, 1984
Beavan, C., *Operation Jedburgh*. New York: Penguin Books, 2014
Bourhill, James, *The Killing Fields of Provence*, Barnsley: Pen and Sword, 2019
Bourne-Paterson, Major Robert, *SOE in France 1941-1945*, Barnsley: Frontline Books, 2016
Buckmaster, Maurice, *They Fought Alone*, London: Biteback, 2014
Cannicott, Stanley, M, *The Journey of a Jed*, Cheddar: Cheddar Valley Press, 1986
Christensen Jan & Atkins, Nigel, *Secret Operations over Occupied Europe*, Barnsley: Airworld, 2024
Clark, Tim and Cook, Nick, *Monopoli Blues*, London: Unbound, 2018
Cooke, P.E. and Shepherd, B., *European resistance in the Second World War*. Barnsley: Pen & Sword Praetorian Press, 2013
Cookridge, E.H., *They Came from The Sky*. London: Corgi Books, 1976
Cooper, Artemis, *Cairo in the War, 1939-1945*, London: Penguin, 1989
Cowburn, B., *No Cloak, No Dagger*. Barnsley: Frontline, 2009
Cruickshank, Charles Greig, *SOE in the Far East*. Oxford: Oxford University Press. 1986
Dear, I., *Sabotage and Subversion*, London: Cassell Military Paperbacks, 2002
Duckett, Richard, The Special Operations Executive in Burma, London: Bloomsbury Academic, 2022
Foot, M.R. D., *SOE in France*, London: British Broadcasting Corporation, 1966
Foot, M.R.D., *SOE: an Outline History of the Special Operations Executive 1940-1946*. London: British Broadcasting Corporation, 1984.
Ford, R., *Steel from the sky: the Jedburgh Raiders, France 1944*. London: Cassell, 2005.
Funk, A.L., *Hidden Ally*. Westport: Praeger, 1992
Hamilton-Hill, D., *S.O.E. Assignment*. London: New English Library, 1975
Hebditch, D., *Covert Radio Agents, 1939-1945: Signals from Behind Enemy Lines*. Barnsley: Pen and Sword Military, 2023.
Irwin, W., *The Jedburghs: The Secret History of the Allied Special Forces, France 1944*. New York: Public Affairs, 2005.
Jackson, Julian, *France, The Dark Years, 1940-1944*, Oxford: Oxford University Press, 2001

James, W., *The Secret History of SOE: the Special Operations Executive, 1940-1945*. London: St Ermin's, 2002.

Jones, Benjamin, F., *Eisenhower's Guerrillas*, New York: Oxford University Press, 2016

Lacey, Jim, Ed. *Great Strategic Rivalries: From the Classical World to the Cold War*. United Kingdom, Oxford University Press, 2016

Lett, B., *SOE's Mastermind*. Barnsley: Pen and Sword Military, 2016.

Michel, Henri, Trans. André Deutsch Ltd, *The Shadow War, Resistance in Europe, 1939-45*, London: History Book Club, 1972

Neve, Andy and Hedges, Mike, *Portsmouth Water, 1857-2007*, Havant: Portsmouth Water Company, 2007

Ogden, Alan, *Tigers Burning Bright, SOE Heroes in the Far East*, London: Bene Factum, 2013

Parker, R., *Burma WW2, Frontline Stories*. Marston Gate: Amazon, 2011.

Rayment, Sean, *Tales from the Special Forces Club*, London: Collins, 2013

Simon, Paul, *Only One Enemy: The Invader*, London: Hodder & Stoughton, 1942

Singlaub, J. and Macconnell, M., *Hazardous Duty*. New York: Summit Books, 1991

Tierno, Monénembo, *The Black Terrorist*. United States, Diasporic Africa Press, 2012

Tillotson, M. Ed., (2011). *SOE and The Resistance*. London: Continuum, 2011

Trofimov, A.E., *A Most Irregular War*, Bicester: evon Press & The Trofimov Literary Estate, 2023

Verlander, H., *My war in SOE*. Keston: Independent Books, 2010.

Wilt, A.F., *The French Riviera Campaign of August 1944*. Carbondale: Southern Illinois University Press, 1981.

FILMS, TELEVISION, RADIO

Baird, Teddy, Dir., *Now It Can Be Told*, 1947

Crichton, Charles, Dir., *Against the Wind*, 1948

Elms, Robert, *Spooks, Spies and Videotapes*, Radio 4, 2015

Frank, Emma, Dir., *Secret Agent Selection*, BBC, 2018 - Also known as *Churchill's Secret Agents - The New Recruits* (Overseas Markets)

Lilley, Harvey, Dir., *The RAF at 100*, BBC, 2018

Ritchie, Guy, Dir., *The Ministry of Ungentlemanly Warfare*, 2024

Zemeckis, Robert, Dir., *Allied*, 2016

WEBSITES

CIA, https://www.cia.gov/stories/story/surprise-kill-vanish-the-legend-of-the-jedburghs/

Legasee, https://www.legasee.org.uk/

Tatton Park, https://www.tattonpark.org.uk/pdf/wwii_information_sheet.pdf

The Secret WW2 Learning Network, https://secret-ww2.net/

U.S. Military Forum, https://www.usmilitariaforum.com/forums/

INDEX

A
Abbasiya, 76
Alcee, Captain R, real name Captain Pierre Bloch, 54, 55, 58, 61, 63, 118
Allen-Mirehouse, Captain Jimmy, 82, 84
Andersen, Sergeant R J, 67
Alexandria, 76–77
Algeria, vii, 42, 54, 118, 133
Algiers, 26, 48, 52–55, 58–59, 62, 66–67, 74, 133, 137, 141, 148
Ansouis, 59
Apt, 55, 58, 60, 63, 137
Archiduc, see also Rayon, Camille, 57, 67
Austin, Captain, 54
Australia, 97, 108–9, 111, 121, 125
Austria, 11, 76–77
Avignon, 60, 64, 68, 75, 77

B
Bailey, Dora, 8
Bailey, Dora, Sr, 8, 10
Bailey, Frederick, Sr, 8
Bailey, Fred, 1–5, 7–11, 16, 21–22, 25, 29, 30–42, 47–49, 51–67, 72–73, 75–77, 81–113, 115–121, 123–132, 136, 146, 148, 150, 172
Bailey, Sheila, 103–106, 108–112, 115, 119, 120, 127, 131
Bailey, Sylvia, 102–103
Bai Maung, Ba Maung/UBau Maung, 82
Balkans, 25, 28
Bank, Aaron, 121
Bari, 75–76
Bartter, Flight Lieutenant Peter, 35
Battersby, Major, 83
BCRA, Bureau Central de Renseignements et d'Action, 16, 44–45, 49, 74
Beaurepaire, 148
Belfort, 60, 159
Belgium, 26, 28
Bentota, 100
Bergé, Georges, 3
Bernard, Roger, 58
Beyne, Commandant, 58
Bezancon, 68
Bilin, 86, 88
Blackwell, Anthony, 10
Blancon, 68
Blida, 55, 66
Bloch, Pierre Captain nom de guerre Alcee, see Alcee
Bo Hon Shwe, 91
Bonner, Major, 69
Bosham, 103–104, 110
Bosham Parish Council, 110
Bovington, 21–22, 25, 93
Brault, G E – 'Jerome', 35
Briancon, 71, 143–144, 145
Brignoles, 70–71, 73
Brittany, 48–50, 156
British Empire Exhibition, 7
Brown, Arthur, 32, 36, 39, 54, 167
Brown, Oscar, 76
Buckmaster, Maurice, 15, 30
Burma, 1, 4–5, 79–82, 85, 93–95, 97, 100, 109, 124–125, 129
Burmese National Army, BNA, 84, 86–88, 91, 94
Buy de Baronies, 67

C
Cadogan, Permanent Under Secretary, 13
Cain, Sergeant 'Cobber' Thomas, 75, 147
Cairo, 76–77
Calcutta, 81–83, 88, 90–91, 93
Cannicott, Stanley, 25

Camp W, *see* El Riath
Cape Town Castle, 42
Carew, Keggie, 4
Carew, Major Tom, 4, 93
Cenotaph, 3, 117
Ceylon, 93, 99
Casey, William, 54
Cavaillon, 60
C G E Tousa (European Theatre of Operations), 25
Chamberlain, Neville, 11, 14
Char, René, 58
Character Operation, *see* Operation Character
Charnwood Forest, 39
Chauknkwa, 87
Chateau de la Vachere, 68
Chateau de Montellier, 68
Chateauneuf du Faou, 50
China, 81
Chinese Guerrillas, 14–15, 98
Chirac, Jacques, 119
Churchill, Winston, 2, 11, 13–14, 23, 76, 123
CIA, 2, 18, 37, 122–123
Clerkenwell, 7
Cloitre, *see* Widmer
Colby, William, 122
Colne Valley Water Company, 10, 102
Colombo Beach, 99
Communist, France, *see also* FTP, 16, 44, 48, 74, 98, 142, 144, 158
Constans, Colonel Jean, 57, 67
Copsey, Robert, 126
Cornick, Sergeant Ted, 75, 142, 149
Corps Franc, 58–60
Corsica, 71, 137
Courthezon, 61, 65
Cox, Major J, 93
Cox, Martyn, 4, 102, 124, 126
Crewe House, 12
Critchley, Colonel, 90, 92
Croix de Guerre, 65, 101, 111, 129
Crosby, Major, 60, 67, 137
Czechoslovakia, 11

D
Dalton, Hugh, 14
Davis, John, 98
De Gaulle, 16, 26, 43–44, 49, 65, 75, 141, 158
De Shayes, 71

Denmark, 35, 118
Dragoon, *see* Operation Dragoon
Duchene, Commandant, 63
Dunbar, 39
Durance, River, 58

E
Eastbourne, 9, 105
Edgar, Sergeant, 82, 84, 91
Eisenhower, 2, 45, 128, 139
Electra House, 12
Eldridge, Sergeant, 96
Ellis, Mary, 125
El Riath, Camp W, 53
Eydoux, Captain, 74

F
F Section, 15, 26, 45, 74–75
Sub sections
 AMF, 26
 DF, 26
 DR/JED, 26
 EU/P, 26
 RF, 16, 26, 45
Fairford Airfield, 48, 52, 156
Fawley Court, 31–32, 35–36
Fayence, 70
Ferandon, Lt F L., 72–73
FFI, Forces Françaises de Interieur, French Forces of the Interior, 48–49, 60, 63, 65, 68, 143, 145–147, 150–154
Firmin, 72
Firestone, 8
Foot, M R. D., 3, 24, 127, 138
Force 136, 5, 35, 77, 79, 81, 83, 94, 99
Ford, Major, 91
Ford Motor Company, 15
Fort Hertz, 81
Foster, Lt R H., 67–69
Frank, Emma, 125
FTP, Franc-Tireurs et Partisans, *see also* Communist, France, 48, 60, 63, 67–68, 138, 140, 144–145, 148
Fuller, Major H W., 34, 134

G
Galvanic, see Operation Galvanic
Gap, 71
Gardner, Sergeant Dennis, 62, 119, 148
Gas Consumers Council, 108
Gendarmerie Maritime, 60
Generich, Lt., 71

INDEX

Gestapo, 40, 69, 159
GHQ Home Forces, 25
Gibraltar, 81
Gosport Water Works, 102
Gough, Captain Victor, 40
Gouzy, Colonel, 72–73
Grand, Colonel Lawrence, 2, 12–13
Grant, Josh, 124
Grasse, 70
Green Berets, 2–3, 119, 121
Green Howards, 21–22, 77
Grenoble, 53, 62, 64, 69, 71, 142, 144–145
GSR, 12
Gubbins, Major General Colin, 2, 14–15, 22–23, 115, 118, 123, 127–128

H
Hackard, 71
Halifax, Lord, 12–13
Hallows, Captain Geoffrey, 76, 137–138
Hankey, Maurice, 13
Hanna, Lt W C., 69–71
Harcourt, Captain R., 56, 70, 72–74
Harrington Airfield, 37, 48, 52, 121, 152
Harrington Aviation Museum, 37
Havant, 102
Hemel Hempstead Grammar, 9
HMS Chitral, 81
Holdsworth, Gerry, 76
Holland, 28, 164–166, 168
Holland, Colonel J F C., 2, 12–13
Hondona, 93, 95
Honfleur, 110
Hong Kong, 2, 79
Hotel Crillon, 64, 75
Hoover, the vacuum company, 8
Hughes, 71

I
Imperial War Museum, 4, 54, 61, 115, 124
India, 12, 14, 81, 100–101
Indian National Army, INA, 84, 88
Indo-China, 60, 77, 93
Inter Services Security Board, 23

J
Jedburgh Teams
  Alan, 150
  Alfred, 51, 151
  Ammonia, 54, 134
  Aubry 51, 153
  Augustus, 51, 129, 153
  Cinnamon, 56–57, 66, 72, 135
  Citroen, 5, 51, 53–55, 64–67, 72, 118, 133, 135–137, 153
  Dodge, 63, 136
  Frederick, 49, 122, 157
  Giles, 50, 158
  Harold, 51, 123, 158, 163
  Monocle, 66–67, 143
  Sceptre, 69, 147
  Quinine, 54, 135, 146, 165
  Veganin, 62, 122, 136, 148
Jedburgh Teams in France, not listed in main body of book, see Appendix
Jedburgh Teams, casualties, see Appendix
Jedburgh Teams, Burma,
  Team Camel, 93
  Team Cow, 82–83, 87, 91–92, 94
  Team Giraffe, 82–84, 87, 91–92
  Team Rabbit, 82
  Team Panda, 83
Jessore, 83, 96
Jones, Benjamin, 47

K
Kajang, 98
Karen, 81, 90, 93–94
Kaulbeck, Major Ronnie, 92
Kehoe, Bob, 30
Khan, Noor Inyat, 3
Killery, Valentine, 80
Kinmongyon, 84
Kin Saw, 82
Koenig, General, 50, 150
Knox, Captain Bernard, 50, 122
Kuala Lumpur, 98
Kyowaing, 91–92

L
La Bastide des Jordains, 58
Labelle, Major nom de guerre Paul, 57
Lamb, Edward Buckton, 8
Laubier, Captain, 67
Lawrence, T E., 11
Laz, 50
Lebel, Captain, 50
Lee, Sergeant B C., 96–97
Legasee, 4, 61, 124
Legion d'honneur, 65, 111, 128
Legrande, Major, 67–69

Leke, 90
Leney, Sergeant Roger, 4, 76, 84, 93, 137–138, 169
Les Baumettes, 60
Leslie, Lt Commander, 86
Lilley, Harvey, 124
Lindsey, John, 108, 111
Liss, 26
Liverpool, 81
Livron, 68–69
Lofthouse, Joy, 125
London, 3, 7–8, 10, 15, 32–33, 36, 43–44, 52, 76–77, 80, 103, 115–118, 150–154, 156–157
London Gazette, 65
Lucas, Major, 86
Ludovic, Captain *see* Lt Peyrassol
Lumieres, 60
Lyons, Gordon, 106
Lyons, 62, 142, 148, 150

M
McAdam, Major, 82, 84, 86, 91–92
McCoull, Major D C 'Paddy', 82, 84–85, 92
McGregor, Colin, 125
McGregor, Ewan, 125
McLallen, Major, 34
MacPherson, Tommy, 76, 146–147
Mackintosh, Lt., 71
Malacca, 95
Manner, Major, 69
Marks, Leo, 32, 35
Marseille, 72–73, 75, 111, 142
Marten, Major Neil, 70, 75, 122, 148
Martin, Jacques, 119, 135
Maurin, Corporal J., 72
Malaya, 5, 79, 95–96, 98, 100–101, 109
M.E. 25, 82–83
Merriman, Dora, (mother), 8, 10
Merriman, Dora (sister), 8
MI (R), 12–14
Milice, 69, 141, 146, 147
Millar, George, 122
Milton Hall, 26, 33, 36, 38–41, 48, 52, 77, 85, 120
Minlwin, 87, 90
Mirehouse, Captain Jimmy Allen-, *see* Allen-Mirehouse
Misson Nartex, 57
Mogaung, 84
Monopoli, 75, 103

Mongoose, *see* Operation Mongoose
Mongoose Blue, 86
Moore, Sub Lt., 82, 84, 86
Montelimar, 61, 68
Morrison, Captain A R G., 96–97
Moulin, Jean, 44
Moulmein, 86
Mount Lavinia Hotel, 99–100
Moyne, Lord, 76–77
Musgrave, Lt Colonel, 34, 36
Mygaungeing, 87

N
Natgyo, 87
Nation, *see* Operation Nation
Naungadok, 90
Northcliffe, 11
Norway, 15

O
Operation Character, 86, 93
Operation Dragoon, 52–53
Operation Galvanic, 96
Operation Mongoose, 86, 90–92
Operation Nation, 82–83, 93–94
Operation Overlord, 48
Operation Spartan, 23–25
Oradour-sur-Glane, 64
Orange Patrol, 97–98
Oriental Mission, 80
OSS (Office of Strategic Services), 2, 24, 27, 29–30, 69, 93, 122
OTC (Officer Training Corps), 25
Ougnon, Major, 74
Oxhey, 8, 10

P
Padeynyo, 84
Palmer, Sergeant, 69–71
Papun, 81
Parks, Daphne, 36
Paul, *see* Labelle
Pavlovitch, Lt., 73
Pearl Harbour, 79
Penang, 95
Perandon, Captain, 70
Perpendicular Circuit, 54, 72
Pertuis, 58, 60–64, 109
Peterborough, 26, 33, 41, 120
Peyrassol, Lt aka Captain Ludovic, 60
Portsmouth Water Company, 102–103, 106–107

Q
Q codes, 31, 36

R
RAF, 23, 34–35, 91, 124–126, 143, 145
RAF Tangmere, 119, 126
Rangoon, 81, 83, 86, 93, 101
Rayon, Camille, see also Archiduc, 57
Reagan, President Ronald, 119
Richardson, Sergeant D J., 97
Ringway, 38–39
Robertson, Squadron Leader, 97
Romans, 69
Roosevelt, President Franklin, 1–2
Rotary, 106, 108, 110–111
Rotary Housing Project, 108, 110
Royal Armoured Corps, 21, 25, 29, 117
Russia, 14

S
Saint Sauveur, see Constains, Colonel Jean
Salween, 83, 86
SAS, Special Air Service, 2–3, 17–18, 24, 49, 54, 152–153, 155–162
Sault, 57
Saw Bali Creek, 83
Scarborough, 21–22, 25, 93
Schmidt, Paul, 35
Seagram, Major Hugh, 81, 93
Seah Tin Toon, 97
Serendah, 97
Section D, 12–13
Seillons, 73
Selangor, 96
Sevenet, Henri, 17
SHAEF, Supreme Headquarters Allied Expeditionary Forces, 45
Sharpe, John, 93, 115, 123
Singapore, 79–80, 95, 100, 109
Singlaub, Jack, 29, 36, 54, 93, 113, 121–122
Sinn Fein, 14–15
Sittang River, 86, 92
Smallwood, Captain John, 41, 54–55, 58–61, 63, 65, 150
SOE, Special Operations Executive, 2–5, 11, 13–18, 21–29, 31–33, 35, 37, 39, 44, 54, 74–76, 80–81, 102, 112, 115–118, 122–123, 125–138, 149, 152
Spanish Irregulars, 14–15
Spartan, see Operation Spartan
Special Forces Club, 112, 115–118, 132
Spooner, LT Colonel F V, 33–34
Stern Group, 76–77
STO, Service du Travail Obligatoire, 45
St Maximin, 72
Station Yak, 83
STS3, 26
STS40, 35
STS51, 39
STS54a, 31
STS101, 80
Stanley, Oliver, 1–2
Starr, George, 17, 134, 139
Stodham Park, 26
Stuart, Sir Campbell, 12
Szabo, Violet, 3

T
Tack, Sergeant Gordon, 50
Tangmere Military Aviation Museum, 120
Tatton Park, 38
Teams see Jedburgh Teams
Team Surrey, 96
Thaton, 82–83, 86, 91
Thomson-Walker, Major, 97
Tossel, Captain J., 67
Toulouse, 74, 139, 141, 151
Tracey, Sergeant T J., 69
Trevenac, Lt F., 69
Trofimov, Captain Aubrey, 92, 121
Turquet, Major, 29

U
Ulu Yam, 96–97
United States, 1–2, 7–8, 18, 30, 52, 117, 119, 123
Utterback, Lieutenant Colonel Mitch, 113
U San Tint, 82

V
Valence, 68–69
Varages, 72–73
Vaucluse, 55
VE Day, 84
Verity, Hugh, 35, 119
Verlander, Harry, 31–32, 37, 41, 51, 100, 121, 123
Villelaure, 59
Vicenzini, Lt., 60

W

Watford, 8–9
Widmer, Colonel Guillaume, aka Cloitre, 57
Wilkinson, Peter, 2, 23
Wiyaw, 88
Wong, Sergeant, 96–97

Y

Yugoslavia, 15

Z

Z Force, 91
Zokala, 84, 86